Best from BOLLYWOOD

Ramesh Dawar

ibs BOOKS (UK)

Dawar, Ramesh
Best from Bollywood

©Publisher
ISBN 978-1-905863-06-8

First edition 2008

Published by
ibs BOOKS (UK)
55, Warren Street, London W1T 5NW
email: sales@ibsbooks.co.uk
www.ibsbooks.co.uk

Printed in India at
Star Print O Bind
New Delhi 110 020

Designed at
Klakriti Production

Index

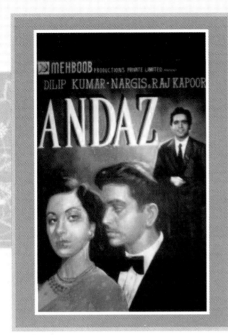

ANDAZ

Andaz 1949

Director	●	Mehboob Khan
Producer	●	Mehboob Productions Ltd.
Starring	●	Nargis................ as Nina
	●	Dilip Kumar......... as Dilip
	●	Raj Kapoor .... as Rajan,
	●	Murad .... as Nina's father,
	●	CuCkoo.............. as Sheila (Nina's
	●	best friend) V.H.Desai, Sapru,
	●	Anwari Bai, Amir Banu, Jamshedji,Wasker.
Music	●	Naushad
Story	●	Shums Luckhnavi
Cinematography	●	Faredoon Irani
Screenplay and dialogue	●	S.Ali Raza
Editing	●	Shamsuddin Kadri
Lyrics	●	Majrooh Sultanpuri
Playback Singers	●	Mukesh, Mohd.Rafi, Lata Mangeshkar
Release date(s)	●	March 21, 1949
Art Direction	●	Keshav Mistry
Language	●	Hindi (B/W)
Sound	●	Kaushik
Concept	●	Social

Andaz presents before the viewer a delightful passion play, unravelling layer by layer the depths of love, jealousy and other complexities that get entwined in a man-woman relationship, often resulting in tragic consequences. *Andaz* was directed by Mehboob Khan

and starred Nargis, Dilip Kumar and Raj Kapoor. In fact, this is the only movie in which the three superstars came together for the first and the last time in a love triangle.

By the time this movie was made, all these three actors were already established in showbiz and commanded great respect for their acting prowess. The two men, Raj Kapoor and Dilip Kumar, were stars in their own rights and as actors they made formidable opponents. In the movie too, their portrayal as antagonists enhanced the dramatic conflict of the story and forced the viewer to sit riveted till the end. Adding to the magic created by these two stars was the brilliant performance by Nargis. She, as rebelliously trendy as ever, plays an entrepreneur, free of gender bias. Her liberal attitude is misread by her business manager (Dilip Kumar), and misconstrued as something more than friendship. And what results from this misunderstanding is a tragic entangle of emotions and feeling from which none can escape unscathed.

Besides these three lead stars, Cukoo and Murad also appeared in the movie in supporting roles.

This layered study of love showcases extraordinarily advanced camerawork by Faredoon Irani. At its time, it was the top grossing Hindi film ever till its record was broken by Raj Kapoor's *Barsaat* in the same year. The music for this film was composed by Naushad and the lyrics were written by Majrooh Sultanpuri.

Memorable songs of 'Andaz'

Song	Singers
Jhoom jhoom ke nacho aaj	Mukesh
Tu kahe agar jeevan bhar main geet sunata jaun	Mukesh
Nigahe bhi mila karti hain, dil bhi dil se milta hai	Mukesh
Hum aaj kahin dil kho baithe	Mukesh
Darna mohabbat karle ulfat mein jholi bhar le	Lata and Shamshad
Koi mere dil mein khushi bankar aaya	Lata
Uthaye jaa unke sitam	Lata
Youn to aapas mein bigadte hain	Lata and Rafi

Nina (Nargis) is the rich and spoilt daughter, the only child, of a rich businessman Sir Badri Prasad (Murad). She is a living symbol of modernism and western aristocracy, and clubs,

ballrooms, golf and riding are her favourite pursuits. She mixes freely with men and is an unhesitating, bold girl.

One day, while horse-riding, she loses control of her horse and is in grave danger. Fortunately, a handsome young man named Dilip (Dilip Kumar) rescues her and saves her from a sudden accidental death. She is grateful to him and their friendship develops. Dilip instantly takes a liking to her and starts to frequently visit her house. With his talented personality and charming manners, Dilip soon becomes an inevitable part of Nina's life. Nina's father dislikes this because she is already committed to another man (Raj Kapoor). He tries to make Nina realise that spending so much time with Dilip is not wise as Dilip could misunderstand her friendship with him for love. Nina promises her father never to do anything to let him down.

Nina's friend, Shiela (Cuckoo) is in love with Dilip, but Dilip's heart is already devoted to Nina. Nina's father suddenly dies of a heart attack and this leaves her devastated. She requests Dilip to manage her business affairs and makes him an equal partner. Dilip is now quite sure that she loves him as well.

Dilip comforts her and tries to reveal his true feelings for her but is shocked by the arrival of Nina's fiancé Rajan (Raj Kapoor) from England. Dilip is surprised that Nina had never mentioned to him that she was already engaged and in love with Rajan. Rajan and Nina eventually get married. Dilip feels cheated and becomes dejected and brooding. When Nina gets married to Rajan, he can restrain himself no longer and reveals all his true feeling for her.

At first, Rajan refuses to suspect his wifes attachment to a stranger. Soon however, suspicion takes hold of him and he is tortured by the thought of Nina's disloyalty. Their marriage cannot survive long against the blow of Dilip's revelation. Rajan begins to suspect Nina at every step and feels sure that she is having an affair with Dilip. He notices that Nina is acting very distant towards him since they got married.

In his rage, Rajan has a fight with Dilip, and thoroughly beats him up. His bitterness and cruelty find expression in hostile and destructive behaviour. What makes this struggle between the two men more interesting is that Nina does after all fall in love with Dilip, though she denies it. She is in a dilemma as she finds herself trapped between two men. Dilip seems to go a little mad, and finally declares his love to Nina, who responds by shooting him dead. She is jailed for murder. She does not regret her action, but rather blames it on her westernised behaviour.

Remarks

- This is the last film made by Mehboob in black and white. This film, its maker, the music director and its stars, all will remain immortal and evergreen in the history of Indian cinema.
- Until 1949, Lata had been a little known singer, when two milestone movies-Mehboob Khan's *Andaz* and Raj Kapoor's *Barsaat* hit the screen. The first song Naushad recorded with Lata Mangeshkar was a duet, the title song of the film, which she rendered with G.M.Durrani.
- In this film Mukesh sings for Dilip Kumar and Mohammed Rafi for Raj Kapoor.

BARSAAT

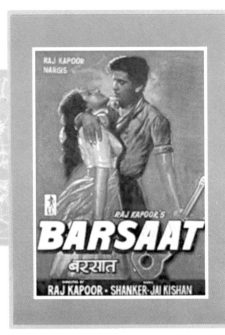

Barsaat 1950

Director	◉	Raj Kapoor
Producer	◉	Raj Kapoor (R.K.Films)
Story, Screenplay and Dialogue	◉	Ramanand Sagar
Starring	◉	Raj Kapoor
	◉	Nargis
	◉	Premnath
	◉	Nimmi
	◉	K.N.Singh
	◉	Cuckoo
Music	◉	Shankar - Jaikishan
Lyrics	◉	Hasrat Jaipuri, Shailendra
Cinematography	◉	Jal Mistry
Art Direction	◉	S.N.Desai
Editing	◉	G. G. Mayekar
Sound	◉	Allaudin
Release date(s)	◉	30th Sept.,1949
Running time	◉	171 min
Playback Singers	◉	Lata Mangeshkar,Mukesh,Mohd.Rafi
Language	◉	Hindi (B/W)

Barsaat   (English translation *Rain*) is the movie that transformed the destiny of Raj Kapoor.   Not only did it gave R.K. Films its famous logo, it was this movie's financial success that enabled Raj Kapoor to buy the R.K. Studios in 1950. It was the first major hit of Raj Kapoor and remains etched in public memory for its romance, performances and unforgettable melodies.

Barsaat is the second film that Raj Kapoor directed. His first directorial film Aag had been only a moderate success at the box office. But Barsaat proved to be a stupendous hit. It stars the famous pair of Raj Kapoor and Nargis as well as Premnath and Nimmi. The romantic and highly sensual posture featuring Nargis and Raj Kapoor became the trademark of R.K. Films. It depicts a young man holding a voilin in one outstretched hand and his lady love arched over his other forearm with her back bent backwards. In that one still frame can be seen all the beauty, love, romance and sensuality that forms an inherent part of all R.K. films.

The muhurat of the film was performed during Dussera, October 1948. People do not know that film was not shot in Kashmir but in Mahableshwar, except the scenic panoramas.

In this film he introduced Ramanand Sagar, Shailendra, Hasrat Jaipuri, Premnath, the doe-eyed Nimmi (Nawab Begum, the daughter of singing star Wahidan Bano of Agra) and music directors Shanker-Jaikishan. The music of Barsaat became an instant hit with the masses. All the songs had a ring of freshness to them and the music was unlike what film-goers had heard until then. The 2 hour-34 minute film had as many as eleven mesmerizing numbers. It was Ramanand Sagar's first film script. The famous playback singer Lata Mangeshkar sang for both Nargis and Nimmi in Barsaat. Until 1949, Lata had been a little known singer. It is believed that the tuneful songs of Barsaat and Mehboob Khan's Andaz truly made her the singing sensation of the era.

All the songs of this movie are memorable and ring with the fragrance of love and the zest of youth.

Memorable songs of 'Barsaat'

Song

Hawa Mein Udta Jaya Mera Lal Dupatta Malmal Ka - Opening number.
Barsaat Mein Humse Mile Tum Sajan - Title song.
Jeeya Bekarar Hai
Chhod gaye balam
Patli Qamer Hai Tirchi Nazar Hai
Mein zindagi mein hardam rota hi raha hoon
Mujhe kissi se pyar ho gaya

Story

The film revolves aound two men, bound together with the fibre of friendship and yet extremely different in temperament, outlook and ideologies. One of the friends, Pran (Raj Kapoor) is rich but sensitive, romantic and idealist. He espouses truth, integrity, fidelity and the meaningfulness of love. Gopal (Prem Nath) on the other hand is flirtatious, a womaniser and a morally uncertain man who equates love with physical desire and fling. He befriends a poor farm girl Neela (Nimmi) during one of his holidays. He makes her believe that he is genuinely in love with her and that even though he has to go back, he would surely return with the rain. Neela believes him and keeps waiting for him.

After some time, he and Pran decide to go on vacation to Kashmir. They stay in a bungalow minded by a poor villager who lives across the mountain stream. But at the time of their visit, he happens to be away from home and since his blind wife cannot take care of the guests, it falls on his daughter Reshma (Nargis) to look after them.

Pran and Reshma soon fall deeply in love. Reshma feels irresistibly drawn towards Pran whenever he plays his viloin. However, when her father returns, he forbids her to meet Pran because he believes that rich, young men from the city only seduce, use and discard the simple village girls.

But one night, when Pran plays a deeply melancholic tune on his violin, Reshma feels once again compelled to go to the house across the stream where Pran is staying. She boards a boat but it sinks as soon as she pushes it into the water. Her father had already broken it to prevent her from escaping to her lover. She tries and struggles to save herself but the turbulent stream sweeps her away.

After the accident, both Pran and Gopal return to the city. Pran is grieving for the sudden demise of his love. Gopal, however, is his normal self and visits nightclubs and enjoys drinking and dancing. Love for him is only the love of body, while far away in the hills, Neela, who loves him with heart and soul, waits for him in sorrow.

Meanwhile, a fisherman (K.N.Singh) from another village finds Reshma unconscious and floating down the mountain stream. He nurses her back to life with the help of a village vaid. He believes that God has sent him a beautiful bride and forces Reshma to get married to him. He takes her to the city to purchase some wedding clothes. There, she hears the same tune on voilin that Pran used to play and rushes into the club, only to find that the voilin player was somebody else. On the marriage day, Reshma tries to run away but the fisherman hauls her back and locks her in his hut.

Gopal decides to go on a holiday again and drags Pran to show him that love can be bought and sold in the open market. He sends Pran into the hut of a young girl in the hills. But Pran sees the pain behind the girl's welcoming smile and finds out that she has been betrayed by a man from the city and she is forced to sell her body to pay for her baby's food and medicines. While returning from the hills, Gopal and Pran hear the wedding music. Pran, who is driving the car, loses control and the car is involved in an accident right in front of the fisherman's hut. The wedding stops half-way as the fisherman comes to help them and takes the wounded Pran into his hut. Here Reshma recognises Pran. The fisherman tries to kill Pran but he is saved by the police at the nick of time. Pran is gravely injured and doctors express fear for her life. Reshma, however, remains strong in her belief that that true love can never die. The doctors operate on Pran in the city hospital and he survives.

All this brings about a change in Gopal's heart too. He now decides to go back to Neela and get married to her, as he had promised her from the very beginning. He takes Pran and Reshma with him to the hills once again. From the hill-top Neela sees Gopal and Reshma walking up to the tourist bungalow arm in arm. She misunderstands their relationship and assumes that Gopal will never come back to her ever again. She is heart broken and life to her seems useless without her love. In sheer dejection, she decides to bring it to an end. When Gopal goes in search of her, she is already dead.

While Pran and Reshma begin their new life, Gopal is left carrying the dead body of Neela to the funeral pyre. The film ends as Neela's body is consumed by the burning fire.

Remarks

◉ In the film when Raj Kapoor and Nargis stare into each other's eyes with longing, they are so fresh, vulnerable and intense that the audience gets deeply engaged in their love story and begins to *feel* the love come alive on screen. What can be more beautiful than love that blossomed in adversity and ended happily ever after.

◉ The depiction of this beautiful love story was supported by no less than eleven songs, well integrated into the story and giving lyrical expression to their romantic sentiments. It touched the heartstrings of the audience, particularly the younger generation, and left them moved.

◉ This film marked the beginning of Raj Kapoor's career as the great showman of Indian cinema.

Awara **1951**

Director	Raj Kapoor	
Producer	Raj Kapoor (R.K.Films)	
Story	Khwaja Ahmad Abbas	
	V.P. Sathe	
Starring	Raj Kapoor..........as	Raj Ragunath
	Nargis.................as	Rita
	Prithviraj Kapoor.as	Judge Raghunath
	Leela Chitnis.......as	Leela Raghunath
	K.N.Singh........... as	Jaggu Daku
	Shashi Kapoor.... as	Young Raj (child artist)
	Cuckoo.................as	Bar dancer
	Helen...................as	Dancer (uncredited)
	Premnath.............as	Cameo appearance in song
	Shashiraj, B.M.Vyas, Baby Zubeida,	
	Honey,O'Brien, Leela Misra, Om Parkash,	
	Rajoo,Mansaram, Rajan, Manek, Paryag	
Distributed by	Esquire Ltd. (Asia)	
Release date(s)	1951	
Running time	193 min	
Language	Hindi/Urdu (B/W)	
Music	Shankar - Jaikishan	

Lyrics	●	Hasrat Jaipuri, Shailendra
Playback Singers	●	Lata Mangeshkar, Mukesh, Mohd.Rafi,
	●	Manna Dey, Shamshad Begum
Camera	●	Radhu Karmakar
Editing	●	G.G.Mayekar
Art Direction	●	M.R.Achrekar
Sound	●	Allaudin

Awara (English translation *The Vagabond*) is the film that immortalised the romantic pair of Raj Kapoor and Nargis. It made the blue-eyed hero a darling of the masses not only

within the country, but all the way to the former Soviet Union. Made in 1951, this film was a collaboration of the famous team of director/producer Raj Kapoor, writer Khwaja Ahmad Abbas, and music composer duo of Shankar-Jaikishan. Its title song '*Awara Hoon*', sung by Mukesh with lyrics by Shailendra, became immensely popular across the Indian subcontinent, as well as in Russia, Romania and China.

The film revolves around the travails of Raj, a poor innocent tramp that endeared himself to one and all by his zest for life, sweet vulnerability and heart of gold. This character, portrayed by Raj Kapoor himself, bears marked resemblance to Charlie Chaplin and was further developed in other Kapoor films such as *Jagte Raho* and *Shri 420*.

The film also stars his real-life father Prithviraj Kapoor as Raj's on-screen father, Judge Raghunath. This was, in fact, the first film in which this father and son combination came together to portray the main characters in the story. Raj Kapoor's youngest brother in real-life, Shashi Kapoor, also featured in the film by playing the childhood version of his character. So did Prithviraj's father Dewan Basheshar Nath Kapoor, who played a cameo role in his only film appearance.

The whole fabric of this classic film is woven around the inter-twining lives of poor Raj (Raj Kapoor) and privileged Rita (Nargis). As the film progresses, a delicate love story is unfolded before the audience through a masterful combination of sensitive direction, brilliant cinematography and songs so melodious and bewitching that they transgressed boundaries of countries as well as time. These songs pulsate with a feeling of love and romance, and even today they manage to flutter the hearts of the young, while generating a feeling of nostalgia among the elderly.

Memorable songs of **'Awara'**

Song	*Singers*
Awara hoon	Mukesh
Dum bhar jo udhar mooh phere	Lata Mangeshkar, Mukesh
Hum tujhse mohabbat karke	Mukesh
Haiyya ho naiyya	Mohammed Rafi
Ek do teen aaja mausam hai Rangeen	Shamshad Begum
Tera bina aag ye chandni	Lata Mangeshkar, Manna Dey
Ghar aaya mera pardesi	Lata Mangeshkar
Aa jao tadapte hai armaan	Lata Mangeshkar
Ek bewafa se pyar kiya	Lata Mangeshkar
Jabse balam ghar aaye	Lata Mangeshkar

Story

Raj is the estranged son of a wealthy but vindictive father (played by Prithviraj Kapoor) who is a district judge. This distance between the father and son resulted from the heinous plan for vengeance carried out by Jaggu (K.N.Singh) who had abducted the judge's wife Bharti (Leela Chitnis) when she was bearing Raj in her womb. Although he let her go unmolested, Judge Raghunath throws her out of his home on suspicion of infidelity. Bharti gives birth to a son in the street with the rain pouring on her. This son grows up to be a tramp named Raj (Raj Kapoor) who is forced to live a life of poverty despite being the son of such an illustrious father. His mother wants him to be an advocate like his father, but Raj is a defiant young man with his own ways and principles. This defiance is very vividly portrayed by the way he secretly ruffles his hair after his mother has neatly oiled and combed it.

The love story of Raj and Rita starts unfolding when, as a child, Raj befriends Rita in school. However, when Rita's parents die, the judge becomes her guardian and tears her away from Raj. He grows up with Rita's memories entrenched deep in his heart.

The young Raj tries to pursue his studies inspite of his dire circumstances. But the money he earns by polishing shoes on the streets of Bombay is not enough and soon he is thrown out of school. Feeling bitter and disappointed, he comes under the influence of Jaggu who leads him to a life of criminality.

While he is engaged in petty crimes, he comes across a rich lawyer

Rita (Nargis) and gets interested in her as a possible prey. But when he discovers that she is his childhood friend, the two start meeting frequently and soon fall in love. He euphemistically tells her, "Rupaye ka len den hi hamara dhanda hai". But Rita awakens Raj's buried feelings of shame at his profession when she teasingly calls him junglee, while gambolling on the beach. In this famous sequence, Raj slaps her ruthlessly. But it instigates a tug-of-war in Raj's conscience, brilliantly expressed in what is cinematically one of the best

dream sequences ever - the twin songs of 'Tere bina aag yeh chaandni' and 'Ghar aaya mera pardesi'. In a surreal recreation of heaven and hell, Raj tries to escape from the hell created by Jaggu.

The film's story takes a dramatic turn when Raj realizes that Jaggu is the man responsible for his mother's banishment from her own home. While attempting to save his mother from the vile clutches of Jaggu, he kills the villain. Later, he also tries to kill the judge, but fails. He is brought to his own father's court, where Rita appears as his lawyer. She examines Judge Raghunath in the witness box. She questions him about his past, about his innocent wife whom he had thrown out of his home, and about the child that was born to her. Judge Raghunath staunchly believes that a thief's son will always be a thief and a good man's son will always turn out good because he carries the blood of his father in his veins. In a series of flashbacks, the film showcases the stormy repercussions of this belief.

Rita, who is aware of the basic innocence of Raj, now throws herself, body and soul into his defence. At last, the truth emerges. Raj is sent to jail for his crime, but Rita promises to wait for him.

The story is told in a very powerful, dramatic style with all the technical flourish possible at that time. The image of the tramp created in this film became so popular that it became a cinematic identity of Raj Kapoor for ever.

Remarks

- The Raj Kapoor-Nargis pair displayed dynamic daring, especially in the scene where Nargis got into a swimsuit for a game on the beach. That scene was performed at a scale of sensuality hit her to unknown to Hindi cinema.
- For the first time in Indian cinema, a very long and unique dream sequence song was picturised in the film. The entire song took three months to shoot.
- Awara created an instant sensation when it was released in 1951. Its fame multiplied

when it was released in Russia as Brodigaya in 1954. The song, 'Awara hoon' echoed across the geographical boundaries. Raj and Nargis were feted wherever they went in Russia.

⊃ After Awara's success, Raj worked exclusively with Nargis for next five years. His next film without Nargis was Sharda (with Meena Kumari) which was made as late as in 1957. Nargis, too, signed films only with Raj Kapoor during this period.

⊃ Awara was the first film to be shot in Raj Kapoor's newly-built R.K. studios. Interestingly, the strains of the tune of 'O basanti pawan pagal' are heard in a couple of scenes in the film. Kapoor used the tune a decade later in Jis Desh Mein Ganga Behti Hai.

⊃ The film grossed over Rs.12 million. This record was beaten the next year by Aan.

Awards

National Award

⊃ The film won the 'Certificate of Merit' at the International Film Festival of India, Bombay in1952

Aan 1952

Director	Mehboob Khan
Producer	Mehboob Khan
	(Mehboob Productions)
Story	R.S.Choudhury
Dialogue	S..Ali Raza
Starring	Dilip Kumar..Jai TilaK
	Premnath ....Shamsher Singh
	Nadira..........Princess Rajshree (debut)
	Nimmi..........Mangala
	Murad...........Maharaja
	Mukri...........Chandan (Jai's friend)
	Cuckoo...........Cameo appearance in Song Sheela
	Nayak, Nilam Bai, Amirbanu.
Music	Naushad
Lyrics	Shakeel Badayuni
Art	M.R.Acharekar
Cinematography	Faredoon A.Irani
Editing	Shamsudin Kadri
Release date(s)	1952
Running time	161 min.
Language	Hindi (Colour)

Aan (English translation *Pride*) was produced and directed by the legendary Mehboob Khan. This romantic adventure not only proved a great success in India but was also much appreciated in the U.K. where it was released with English sub-titles and was called *The Savage Princess*.

Aan was Mehboob Khan's first technicolour spectacle showcasing a lengthy melodrama with lavish sets and a romantic love story of kings and queens, princes and princesses, heroes and knaves, all set in a spectacular mythical kingdom. It was a big budget extravaganza that thrilled the audience and introduced Indian filmgoers to costume fantasy films.

The film starred Dilip Kumar, Nimmi, Premnath and Nadira. It was a debut film for Nadira, a Baghdadi Jewish girl from Nagpada, Bombay. It is however said that initially Nargis was offered the leading role in this film but she did not agree because of her commitment with Raj Kapoor's film *Awara*.

Aan was the first Indian film that used a fight composer. Mehboob Khan introduced Fight Master Azimbhai to supervise the fight sequences in the film. The *muhurat* of this film was performed on October 26, 1949. During the shooting of this film one studio worker died and Nadira too had an accident when she slipped into the water at the Wilson Dam while shooting for the song '*tujhe kho diya ham ne*'.

The movie was not only a thrilling costume drama but a musical blockbuster as well. All the songs of this movie became hit and contributed greatly to the success of the movie. Music director Naushad used his 100 piece orchestra in the film, making the music of this film a memorable experience.

Memorable songs of 'Aan'

Song	Singers
Gaao tarane man ke	Shamshad, Lata and others.
Aaj mere man mein sakhi bansuri bajaye koi	Lata and others.
Mohabbat choomein jinke haath	Mohd. Rafi.
Aag lagi tan man mein dil ko pada thamna	Shamshad Begum.
Dil mein choopa ke pyaar ka toofan le chale	Mohd. Rafi.
Maan mera ehsaan arye naadan	Mohd. Rafi.
Tujhe kho diya hamne paane ke baad	Lata.
Khelo rang hamare sang aaj din rang rangeela aaya	Shamshad, Lata and others.

Story

The film revolves around the story of a royal Indian family that consists of the *Maharaja* (Murad), *Prince* Shamsher Singh (Premnath) and *Princess* Rajshree (Nadira). They are the absolute monarchs of the region and are much revered.

Prince Shamsher becomes enraged when the Maharaja reveals that Shamsher will not be the heir to his throne after his death. Shamsher plans to gain control of the kingdom by killing the Maharaja on the night before he is due to travel to England for medical treatment. However, he is unsuccessful. Maharaja escapes the attempt on his life by Shamsher's henchmen and disguises himself as a servant in his own palace. Shamsher announces to the world that the king, his father, is dead and assumes control over the throne and the region.

A poor villager named Jai Tilak (Dilip Kumar) enters a contest to tame Princess Rajshree's wild horse. He wins the contest but instead of being pleased with him Princess Rajshree and Prince Shamsher are angered that a poor villager has managed to defeat them. Jai falls in love with the princess and tries numerous times to woo her. Shamsher uses his powers as a force of oppression, and increases the taxes on the already struggling and poverty-stricken people. Jai Tilak becomes the leader of the fight against this oppression.

Mangala (Nimmi) is a village girl and childhood friend of Jai. She loves Jai but her love is not reciprocated by him as he loves the Princess instead. Mangla catches Shamsher's eye. He kidnaps her and tries to rape her causing her to fall to her death. In retaliation, Jai manages to kidnap Rajshree. He sets out to gain her love by taking her into his village. He teaches her the ways of living as a village peasant girl so that she realises what poverty is. Just when Rajshree begins to realise her feelings for Jai, Shamsher Singh returns to get his revenge against Jai. Meanwhile, it is revealed that the king is alive, so Jai, Rajshree and the loyal clansmen come together to defeat Shamsher and restore the king to the throne.

Remarks

- The film was the highest grosser of 1952 and was the first to gross over Rs.15 million. This record was beaten 3 years later by *Shree 420* in 1955.
- The film was considered to be rarity in Bollywood at that time as it was made in the style of the costume fantasy films such as *The Thief of Bagdad*.
- It was released with English sub-titles outside India under the title of *The Savage Princess*. The world premiere was held in London, on August 1, 1952.
- Mehboob became one of the first in Indian films to experiment with colour in *Aan*.

Baiju Bawara **1952**

Director	○	Vijay Bhatt
Producer	○	Prakash Pictures
Story	○	R.S. Choudhury (screenplay)
	○	Zia Sarhadi (dialogue)
	○	Ramchandra Thakur (story)
Starring	○	Meena Kumari..........Gauri
	○	Bharat Bhushan.......Baij Nath 'Baiju'
	○	Surendra..................Tansen
	○	Kuldip Kaur..............Roopmaji
	○	Bipin Gupt................Akbar
	○	Manmohan Krishna..Shankar Anand
	○	B.M. Vyas................Mohan
	○	Mishra......................Narpat
	○	Radhakrishan...........Ghasit Khan
	○	Kesari.......................Ganjoo
	○	Ratan Kumar............Young Baiju
	○	Tabassum.................Young Gauri
	○	Rai Mohan................Swami Haridas
	○	Bhagwanji................Baiju's Father
	○	Nadir.......................Hajhi Singh
Music	○	Naushad

Lyrics	✪	Shakeel Badayuni
Cinematography	✪	V.N. Reddy
Editing	✪	Pratap Dave
Release date(s)	✪	1952
Language	✪	Hindi (B/W)
Running time	✪	165 min

Baiju Bawra is a musical classic directed by Vijay Bhatt. It starred Bharat Bhushan and Meena Kumari. Meena Kumari's role as Gauri in this movie was her first major role on screen.

Baiju Bawra is the story of one of India's greatest exponents of classical music. It revolves around Baiju, a young singer in the time of the Mughal Emperor, Akbar, who sets out to avenge his father's death. It is considered by some as the sweetest musical film ever produced.

Since the plot centred on music, it was necessary that the movie's soundtrack be outstanding. Legendary music director Naushad and lyricist Shakeel Badayuni more than lived up to the challenge. All the songs from the movie were based on Hindustani classical tunes or *ragas*. Mohammad Rafi, Lata Mangeshkar, and Shamshad Begum lent their voices to the score. The result was one of the most critically-acclaimed musicals of Hindi cinema

Memorable songs of 'Baiju Bawra'

Song	*Singers*
Tu ganga ki mouj	Lata Mangeshkar and Mohd. Rafi.
Mohe bhool gaye sanwariya	Lata Mangeshkar.
Bachpan ki mohabbat ko	Lata Mangeshkar.
Door koi gaye dhun ye soonaye	Lata Mangeshkar, Mohd.Rafi, Shamshad Begum and others.
Man tarpat hari	Mohd.Rafi,
Aaj gaawat man mer	D.V. Palusker and Aamir Khan.
O duniya ke rakhwale	Rafi.
Jhoole mein pawan ki Aayi bahar	Lata Mangeshkar and Rafi.

The film is based on the legend of Baiju Bawra from the era of Mughal Emperor Akbar. Baiju (Bharat Bhushan) is the innocent son of a musician who grows up to be a singer himself. He is a disciple of Swami Haridas and lives in a pastoral surrounding on the banks of the river Jamuna. When his father is killed by Akbar's men for singing outside Tansen's palace, Baiju believes that Tansen, the famed court musician of Emperor Akbar, is responsible for his father's death and vows to take revenge. In pursuit of his vengeance, he goes to a small village on the banks of river Jamuna, where he meets Gauri (Meena Kumari), a village belle. He falls in love with Gauri who is a daughter of a boatman. He likes singing to his beloved Gauri, while she sits on a swing in a bower of flowers. However, in pursuance of his desire to kill Tansen, Baiju leaves her and goes in search of the great musician. But he is unable to think of killing when he hears Tansen singing. Tansen tells him that he can be vanquished only by music. So Baiju attempts to avenge his father's death by challenging Tansen in a musical duel.

Meanwhile, Gauri, to escape a forced marriage, comes in search of Baiju and is attacked by a snake. Baiju goes mad when he discovers this, and when he gets the chance to compete with Tansen, he is not able to sing. But a second chance comes to him, and this time Baiju defeats Tansen in a musical duel in the court of Akbar. In the film, even the statue weeps when Baiju sings in sorrow 'O Duniya ke rakhwaale'.
Baiju rushes back to the village to stop Gauri's wedding, but when he wants to cross the river the boatman refuses to take him across. Baiju plunges into the river Jamuna and drowns. When Gauri hears of his death, she too embraces death and leaves the world to join him in his eternal abode.

Awards

Filmfare Awards

- Meena Kumari for her performance
- Naushad for his music

Do Bigha Zameen 1953

Director	◎	Bimal Roy
Producer	◎	Bimal Roy Productions
Story	◎	Salil Choudhury (story)
	◎	Paul Mahendra (dialogue)
	◎	Hrishikesh Mukherjee (scenario)
Starring	◎	Balraj Sahni …as Shambhu
	◎	Nirupa Roy …..as Parvati
	◎	Ratan Kumar, Murad, Jagdeep, Nana Palsikar
	◎	Nasir Hussain, Kusum
	◎	Dilip (Junior), Mehmood, Meena Kumari (Guest)
Music	◎	Salil Choudhury
Lyrics	◎	Shailendra
Cinematography	◎	Kamal Bose
Art:	◎	Gonesh Basak
Editing	◎	Hrishikesh Mukherjee
Distributed by	◎	Shemaroo Video Pvt.Ltd.
Release date	◎	1953
Running time	◎	142 min
Country	◎	India
Language	◎	Hindi (B/W)

Do Bigha Zameen (English translation *Two Bighas of land*) is a Hindi movie directed by Bengali director Bimal Roy. The film has a heavy socialist theme, and belongs to the

parallel cinema tradition. In this movie the plight of a poor farmer, caught in the vicious grip of money lenders, is brought alive by the highly effective performance of Balraj Sahni. In fact, his portrayal of Shambhu is considered as one of his best performances ever.

Like other movies by Roy, art and commercial cinema are exquisitely merged to produce a movie that is still looked upon as a benchmark.

Memorable songs of 'Do Bigha Zameen'

Song	Singers
Hariyala sawan dhol bajata aaya	Lata , Manna De and others
Ajab tere duniya ho more rama	Mohd.Rafi and others
Aa jaa ree aa nindiya tu aa	Lata

Story

The movie is placed in the year 1953, and an annual drought is shown ravaging through the state of West Bengal. Small farmers, living at the mercy of nature, are caught between an unpredictable monsoon on one hand and landlords and moneylenders charging high rates of interest on the other.

The story revolves around a farmer, Shambhu (Balraj Sahni), who has been hit badly by the famine on rampage in Bengal. The two acres of land that he owns is his only wealth. He has no money; even his wife's jewellery is in the clutches of a pawn shop. All he can do is to hope for the mercy of nature, because there is never any question of expecting mercy from a *zamindar* or a pawn dealer.

To make matters worse, the *zamindar* (land owner) wants to acquire Shambhu's land on the pretext of non-repayment of the loan Shambhu had taken from him. The zamindar wants to sell the village land to a city contractor to build a factory. Shambhu refuses to sell his land, but zamindar threatens to forcibly occupy the land if he does not return the money within a day. The court, however, grants him a three month period to return the money. Shambhu moves to the city with his son in hope of finding some way to earn so much money in so little time.

They are robbed of all their possessions on the very first night of their stay in Calcutta. However, they remain determined to live in the city and earn enough money to save their land. Shambhu takes to pulling a rickshaw while his son Kanhaiya (Ratan Kumar) polishes shoes. They face illness, injury and other hardships but go on unremittingly labouring to save their precious land. Their day revolves around earning money and counting their savings. But the money coming in is too little, and too slow. Kanhaiya even steals money to help his father. But Shambhu would not accept the stolen money and is furious at his son.

The most famous scene from the film is when Shambhu pushes himself to the limit pulling his rickshaw. The rider on the rickshaw offers Shambhu more money to pull faster because he is chasing his girlfriend in another rickshaw. Shambhu cannot resist the temptation. He makes himself run faster and faster, his strength failing but a smile lighting up

in his eyes in anticipation of getting more money. Typically, his wealthy customer is not at all worried about his plight. In this race, Shambhu's rickshaw loses a wheel and he gets gravely injured.

Meanwhile, not having heard anything from her husband and son, Shambhu's worried wife Parvati (Nirupa Roy) comes to Calcutta in search of them. While trying to save her son from the clutches of city's bad elements, she getsrun over by a car. Fortunately, Shambhu finds her lying on the road and gets her admitted into a hospital. Kanhaiya, in his mother's presence, tears up the money he has stolen.

The movie clearly depicts that even while battling with all these bitter hardships, Shambhu does not lose his righteousness, and remains an honest man even in the face of adversity. This is the moral of the film. Shambhu's morality is the only thing that remains his own till the end.

When they return to their village, they see a huge factory being raised on their land. Shambhu has lost everything. And he is not even allowed to take a handful of earth from the land that was once his.

Awards

- *Do Bigha Zameen* won the International Prize at the Cannes Film Festival-Grand Prix (1954) and Prize for Social Progress Karlovy Vary (54).
- The movie won the first ever Filmfare award in 1954. Bimal Roy won the filmfare award as the best director.
- The movie also won the first President's award All India Certificate of merit now known as National Film Awards.

Theme

- The troubles and the turmoil that befalls the main character Shambhu, demonstrate the condition of poor farmers in pre-independence (and early post independence) India. The society of the time was agrarian and the farmers were poor. This poverty was mainly due to the fact that most farmers had very small land holdings and were uneducated. They were gullible and fell easy prey to land owners, money lenders, and the Brahmins who were cunning and selfish. During that time, many people moved to the cities, either in anticipation of gaining fortunes, or because they could not survive the atrocities of power holders. The movie has a theme that can be found in the works of notable Indian authors of the era like Munshi Premchand or Sarat Chandra Chattopadhyay.
- Despite the many awards that the movie received, it is sometimes criticized in modern times, due to its portrayal of the rich as arrogant and the poor as unquestionably moralistic. But in the 1950s, films based on post-Independence India tended to have socialist themes and were in fact quite popular throughout the world, especially in Russia, Greece and China. In such countries there was a huge population of poor and films like *Do Bigha Zameen* found a sympathetic audience and were consequently well received. It was widely regarded in its time as a milestone in Indian Cinema. Despite the use of songs and occasional plot, the film has simplicity and a genuineness which makes it memorable. The film was not only successful in India but won several International Awards as well.

Title

- The name of the movie means "Two Bigha of Land." *Bigha* is a unit of measuring land. Bigha varies from state to state. In Bengal, where the movie is based, 3 bigha is one acre (4,000 m²). Accordinly, Shambhu owned only 2,700 m² of land in this story

Boot Polish 1954

Director	●	Prakash Arora
Producer	●	Raj Kapoor (R.K.Films)
Story, Screenplay and Dialogue	●	Bhanu Pratap
Lyrics	●	Hasrat Jaipuri, Shailendra and Deepak
Sound	●	Shankar Amruta
Starring	●	Baby Naaz
	●	Ratan Kumar, Budho Advani
	●	Prabhu Arora, David
	●	Chand Burque, Veera
	●	Bhupendra Kapoor, Shailendra
Music	●	Shankar-Jaikishan
Art Director	●	M.R.Achrekar
Cinematography	●	Tara Dutt
Singers	●	Asha Bhonsle, Mohd. Rafi
	●	Talat Mahmood, Manna De
Editing	●	G. G. Mayekar
Release date(s)	●	1954
Running time	●	149 min.
Country	●	India
Language	●	Hindi (B/W)

Boot Polish (English translation *Shoe Shine*) is a poignant tale of two poverty stricken children striving to live a life of honesty and pride. Thanks to the powerful performances by both the child artists, the film touched the hearts of many and made the audience comprehend the daily travails faced by countless children forced to spend their lives on the streets.

This was the first film based on the need for eradication of begging in India. It contained a socially significant message that was appreciated by all. Raj Kapoor, like in his earlier films, used the medium of cinema as a means of raising the social consciousness of the people and calling attention to the evils that exist in our society and stand in the way of progress. *Boot Polish* has a clear social reformist content and humanistic approach. The delicate handling of the theme and the powerful story built around it forced many to ponder and act for the social cause brought out in the film.

The tuneful music of the film received all round appreciation. The songs, which were imbued with the innocence and sweetness of childhood, became hugely popular especially among children.

Memorable songs of 'Boot Polish'

Song	*Singers*
Nanhe Munnhe Bachche Teri Mutthi Mein Kya Hai	Rafi, Asha and others
Thair Zara O Zane wale Babu Mister Gore Kale	Manna De and Asha
Chalee Kaun Se Desh Gujaria Too Sajh Dhaj Ke	Asha and Talat Mahmood
Tumhare Hain Tumse Dua Mangte Hain	Rafi, Asha and others

Story

Boot Polish is a story of two orphans struggling for their very survival in the city of Bombay on the shores of the Arabian Sea. Hidden behind the glitter of this city, there are slums where people are suffering from poverty and pursue an endless struggle for their livelihood. The story of this film revolves around two such destitutes.

Little Bhola and his younger sister Belu are very poor. They live in one of the slums of Bombay. The lane where they live is dirty and narrow and crowded with other beggars and petty criminals. The two children have been trained in the art of begging by a distant relative, Kamla Chachi. She is a woman of dubious character. The children are forced to spend their miserable lives in her dilapidated cottage. She beats and abuses them at the slightest mistake. But they get sympathy and hope of their good future from their neighbour John Chacha (David), an old eccentric bootlegger who is kind hearted and a straight forward man. He teaches the children that working and earning with their own hands is more dignified than begging.

Goaded by John Chacha, the children decide to give up begging and become shoeshiners. Unfortunately, when Bhola and Belu are settling down in their new job, John is taken away by the police. Unkind and rude Kamla Chachi becomes furious on the children for giving up begging which used to bring her more money. She turns them out from her cottage. It's a rainy day and the children can find no customers for polishing their shoes. They move from one place to another in search of customers, but are disappointed

Belu is so hungry that she pleads with her brother to beg again, so that they may buy some food. Bhola is very disturbed. His dear sister is starving but he has taken a vow not to beg again.

But the night, no matter how long it is, must end finally and the bright dawn is never far away. Bhola, Belu and John meet again on the crossroads of life. The miseries and hardships are left behind and a new life begins for all of them. It's a life of love, hope, regard and self-respect.

 Remarks

○ Though the film was produced by Raj Kapoor (R.K.Films), it was directed by Prakash Arora. This was the time when Raj Kapoor encouraged his assistants to become full fledged directors under his guidance in order to diversify his production company.

Awards

- Asian Film Festival -1955
- Grand Prix for Music for Shankar- Jaikishan
- Cannes International film festival (France)-1955
- Special Mention to the child actress Baby Naaz
- Prakash Arora was nominated for the Golden PalmSouth East

Filmfare Awards

- Best Cinematographer - Tara Dutt
- Best Film - Raj Kapoor
- Best Supporting Actor - David Abraham

Mirza Ghalib

MIRZA GHALIB

Mirza Ghalib 1954

Director	●	Sohrab Modi
Producer	●	Sohrab Modi (Minerva Movietone)
Story	●	Rajinder Singh Bedi
Sadat Hasan Manto (story)	●	J.K. Nanda
Starring	●	Bharat Bhushan
	●	Suraiya
	●	Nigar Sultana
	●	Durga Khote
	●	Murad, Mukri
	●	Ulhas, Kumkum
	●	Iftekhar, Sadat Ali
	●	Roshan, Jagdish Sethi
Music	●	Ghulam Mohammed
Choreography	●	Lachhoo Maharaj
Sound	●	M.Edulji
Art	●	Rusi K.Banker
Cinematography	●	V. Avadhut
Screenplay	●	J.K.Nanda
Release date(s)	●	1954
Running time	●	145 min.
Language	●	Hindi / Urdu (B/W)

Mirza Ghalib (1954) is a Hindi/Urdu film, directed by Sohrab Modi. It is based upon the life of well known poet Mirza Ghalib. It stars Bharat Bhushan as Ghalib and Suraiya as his courtesan lover. The film won the President's Gold Medal for Best Feature Film at the National Film Awards in 1955.

Memorable songs of 'Mirza Ghalib'

Song	Singers
Nuktachi hain gham-e- dil, unko soonaye na bane	Suraiya
Hain bas ki har ek unke ishare mein nishan aur	Mohd. Rafi
Phir mujhe deedaye tar yaad aaya	Talat Mahmood
Dil-e- nadan tujhe hooaa kya hai	Talat Mahmood andSuraiya
Aah ko chahiye ek umar asar hone tak	Suraiya
Rahiye ab ayesi jagah chal kar jahan koi na ho	Suraiya
Yeh na thi hamari kismat ki visale yaar hota	Suraiya
Chali Pee ke nagar, ab kahe ka dar	Shamshaad Begum and others

Story

The film depicts the life of the nineteenth century Urdu poet Mirza Ghalib (Bharat Bhushan), who lived during the reign of Bahadur Shah Zafar, the last of the Mughal emperors.

At a symposium at the court of Bahadur Shah Zafar, Ghalib's poetry fails to impress an audience steeped in the traditional form of *Ghazal*. Disheartened, he leaves the court. On his way home, he overhears someone singing his verses. Seeking to find the singer, he discovers Moti Begum (Suraiya) who is an ardent fan of his poetry.

Ghalib falls in love with Moti Begum who is a beautiful courtesan. He renames her '*Chaudhvi*' However, his association with her offends many, including the Kotwal. Ghalib loses contact with Moti due to a misunderstanding and the film revolves around his trials,

successes and failures as well as the ultimate descent of this wealthy and noble poet into poverty.

Moti, still in love with Ghalib, sings one of his verses to the emperor to remind him of Ghalib's pitiable condition. The emperor, charmed, does honour him, but the crooked Kotwal is not done yet and has Ghalib imprisoned on gambling charges. By the time Ghalib is released, Moti Begum is too ill and dies in his arms.

Remarks

● Pandit Jawaharlal Nehru, who was the Prime Minister of India at the time of the film's release, after seeing the film, complimented Suraiya by saying, *"you have brought Mirza Ghalib to life"*.

Awards

National Award

- President's Gold Medal - Best Feature Film
- President's Silver Medal

Devdas 1 9 5 5

Director	○	Bimal Roy
Producer	○	Bimal Roy Productions
Story	○	Based on Sarat Chandra Chattopadhyay's Novel
	○	Script for the film by Rajinder Singh Bedi
Starring	○	Dilip Kumar.......... as Devdas
	○	Suchitra Sen..........as Parvati (Paro)
	○	Vyjayanthimala......as Chandramukhi
	○	Motilal..................as Chunni Babu
	○	Nasir ussain...........as Dharamdas
	○	Murad...................as Devdas' father
	○	Kanhaiyalal ....as Teacher
	○	Iftekhar................ as Bhijudas
	○	Shivraj .... as Nilkant (Parvati'sfather)
	○	Nana Palsikar .... as Street Singer
	○	Moni Chatterji, Ashim Kumar, Ram Kumar
	○	Vikram Kapoor, Ved, Pran
Music and Lyrics	○	Sachin Dev Burman
Cinematography	○	Kamal Bose
Screenplay	○	Nabendu Bose
Release date(s)	○	1955
Art	○	Sudhendu Roy

Editing	Hrishikesh Mukherji
Running time	159 min
Language	Hindi (B/W)

Devdas (Hindi) is a 1955 film based on the adaptation of Sarat Chandra Chattopadhyay's classic novel about a self-absorbed hero who destroys his own happiness in pursuit of love. *Devdas* is perhaps the most widely read novel of Indian literature. It's not surprising therefore, that till now there have been as many as seven film versions of *Devdas* in various Indian languages, including a silent movie in 1928.

Bimal Roy's *Devdas* is an unforgettable film. Kamal Bose's exquisite black and white photography captures the essence of the theme beautifully. All the songs were written and composed by Sachin Dev Burman and and were very popular

Memorable songs of '**Devdas**'

Song	Singers
Kisko Khaber Thi Kisko Yakin Tha	Talat Mahmood
Jise Tu Kabool Kar Le	Lata Mangeshkar
O Albele Panchi Tera Door Thikana Hai	Asha and Usha Mangeshkar
Aan Milo Aan Milo Shyam Sanvre	Geeta Dutt and Manna De
O Jane Wale Rukja Koi Dam	Lata Mangeshkar
Vo Na Aange Palat Kar	Mubarak Begum

Story

Devdas (Dilip Kumar) and Parvati or Paro (Suchitra Sen) are childhood playmates, deeply attached to each other. They grow up in a small village with a love-hate relationship that matures into a deep and intense love when they grow older. However, consideration of caste and family pride come in the way of fulfillment of this love. Devdas comes from a very rich and wealthy family. Parvati is a daughter of their poor neighbours. His father does not approve of his marriage or even any friendship with Paro, and sends him away to Calcutta to finish his education.

Vyjayantimala with Dilip Kumar

Devdas fails to take a bold stand to marry Paro against his father's wishes. He gives up on his love, and Paro gets married to a much older but wealthy widower Zamindar of a nearby district, who has a grown-up son and daughter from his earlier marriage.

However, Devdas soon realizes that life would be meaningless without the love of Paro. He returns to the village but by that time she's already married. He can do nothing now to bring back his lost love. He goes back to Calcutta with a broken heart and falls into bad company. One night he is persuaded to drink liquor by his friend Chunilal (Motilal). Chunilal also introduces him to a dancer, Chandramukhi (Vyjayantimala), who adores him and falls hopelessly in love with him. Devdas in not aware of Chandramukhi's affection and love for him, as most of his time is spent in an alcoholic stupor, and he cannot get over his love for Parvati.

Time passes and Parvati comes to know of Devdas' ruin. She finds him and tries to wean him away from his drinking. He promises her that before he dies, he will seek her out for help. She goes back to her home and tries to attain the Hindu ideals of a dutiful wife. In the final hours of his terminal illness, Devdas takes a last journey to his love's abode. After traveling all night in a very sick condition, he reaches at Parvati's door-step but can go no further. Death meets him before his love.

The police enquiries prove that the body lying at the doorstep of the Zamindar is of Devdas. Behind the high surrounding walls of her home, Parvati hears that her beloved is dead, and she also breaks down.

Remarks

◦ Initially, Nargis and Meena Kumari were considered for the role of Devdas's childhood sweetheart Parvati. However, it was Suchitra Sen who was finally selected.

Awards

Filmfare Awards

◦ Best Actor Award to Dilip Kumar
◦ best Actress Award to Vyjayanthimala

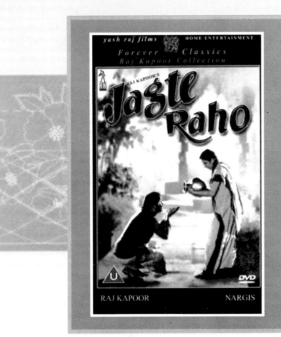

Jagte Raho 1956

Director		Amit Moitra Sombhu Mitra
Producer		Raj Kapoor (R.K.Films)
Story		K.A.Abbas Amit Moitra Sombhu Mitra
Starring		Raj Kapoor, Nargis. Motilal, Pradip Kumar, Sumitra Devi
		Sulochana Chatterjee, Smriti Biswas, Daisy Iran,
		Pahari Nemo,Nana Palsikar
		Sanyal Iftekhar, Pran, S.Banerjee, Bhupendra Kapoor,
		Rashid Khan
Music		Salil Choudhury
Lyrics		Shailendra, Prem Dhawan
Cinematography		Radhu Karmakar
Art Direction		M.R.Achrekar
Editing		G.G.Mayekar ,Vasant Sule
Sound		Allaudin
Distributed by		R.K.Films Ltd
Release date		1956
Running time		149 min
Language		Hindi/Bengali (B/W)

Jagte Raho (English translation *Stay Awake*) was directed by Amit Mitra and Sombhu Moitra, and produced by Raj Kapoor, who also played the lead role. The film centres on the trials of a poor villager (Raju) who comes to the city in search of a better life. However, the naive man soon becomes trapped in a web of middle-class greed and corruption.

The movie is a biting satire depicting the hypocrisy, selfishness and unkindness riddling the so called civilized society. The various ills that remain hidden behind a dark curtain are mercilessly uncovered one by one as the hero of the film, a poor peasant, runs from one door to the other trying to escape the mob following him. It is a story of a dark night, but the light of hope shines in the end. Humanity, it is shown, is not all dead. It still thrives in some hearts, like in the innocence of a little girl and the kindness of the woman who finally quenches the poor man's thirst. And it is in these few people that the hope of a better tomorrow lies.

It is undoubtedly one of the best films of its time where the hard life of a villager is presented in a realistic manner on screen. It is known for its brilliant satire and remarkable acting performance by Raj Kapoor.

The film also features a cameo by Nargis in the final scene. Raj and Nargis team is known to give screen romance a new dimension. They starred in 16 films together. In fact, their association lasted till *Jagte Raho*. After that, they never worked together again.

Besides its brilliant acting, the music of the film is also the highlight of this movie. The songs of *Jagte Raho* are still very popular with people of that generation. Lyrics for the movie were penned by Shailendra and Prem Dhawan and music was composed by Salil Choudhary.

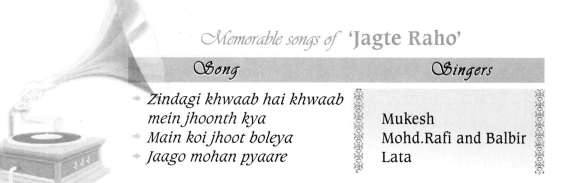

Memorable songs of **'Jagte Raho'**

Song	Singers
Zindagi khwaab hai khwaab mein jhoonth kya	Mukesh
Main koi jhoot boleya	Mohd.Rafi and Balbir
Jaago mohan pyaare	Lata

Story

The entire story takes place in the course of one night. It's a story of an honest, simple and poor young peasant, Raju (Raj Kapoor), who comes from a village to the city of Calcutta in search of work.

It is midnight and Raju is looking for some drinking water to quench his thirst. While roaming around in quest of water, he meets an unsympathetic policeman and a drunkard on  the road. His inherent honesty is brought out when he picks up the purse of the drunk man, which has fallen by the roadside and returns it to him.

His clothes are dirty and in tatters. He has a shaggy, unkempt beard and bewildered, frightened eyes. His lips are parched with thirst. He is desparately searching for some water to drink. He sees a dog entering through the iron grill of the gate at the entrance of a building and drinking water from the dripping tap. Following the dog's example, he too enters the compound of the middle-class housing complex and tries to drink some water. In the streets, the night-watchman shouts *Jaagte Raho* (keep awake).

Raju's appearance and his attitude reflect a certain hesitation and he is mistaken for a thief by the passing policeman. Disturbed by the policeman's shouts, the residents of the apartment building come out and chase him. The windows fly open and the residents raise a hue and cry in the night, calling him a thief. He runs from one apartment to the other trying to escape. While doing so, he witnesses many shady acts in the flats he hides in. Ironically, these crimes are being committed by the so called respectable citizens of the city who lead a life by the day totally in contrast to their night-time deeds behind closed doors. In fact, all are involved in various immoral and nefarious activities. The city is depicted as a den of incredible viciousness, selfishness and cruelty.

Raju is shocked by these events, and tries to escape by evading the search parties that are patrolling the apartment building in search of the elusive thief. He is unfortunately seen, and people chase him to the roof of the building. He puts up a brave resistance and is eventually forced to raise his voice against the victimization. He descends by the water pipes onto the porch of a flat. He goes in and meets a young girl (Daisy Irani). She talks to him kindly and kindles a sense of self-belief in the poor peasant which gives him the strength and determination to face the adversity waiting outside. But when he ventures out of the flat, he's surprised to find that nobody takes notice of him. He knows that the dark night will end, and with the dawn will be born a new day when truth and justice shall prevail. He eventually leaves the apartment building, his thirst still unquenched. He hears a beautiful song and searching for its source arrives at the doorstep of a woman (Nargis) drawing water from a well. His thirst is finally quenched when this woman offers the thirsty tramp the water of life while humming the beautiful song *Jaago Mohan Pyaare*.

Awards

- A shortened version of the film won the Grand Prix at the Karlovy Vary International Film Festival in Czechoslovakia in 1957
- The Union Government of Burma, Rangoon Award on the release of film in 1958.

Do Aankhen Barah Haath **1957**

Director	❷	V.Shantaram
Producer	❷	Rajkamal Kalamandir
Starring	❷	ShantaraM............as Adinath, Jail warden
	❷	Sandhya ....as Champa
	❷	Ulhas, B.M.Vyas
	❷	Baburao Pendharkar
	❷	Paul Sharma,
	❷	Keshavrao Date,
	❷	S.K.Singh.
Music	❷	Vasant Desai
Lyrics	❷	Bharat Vyas
Screenplay	❷	G.D.Madgulkar
Camera	❷	G.Balakrishna
Sound	❷	Mangesh Desai
Release date(s)	❷	1957
Language	❷	Hindi (B/W)

Do Aankhen Barah Haath is a story of a jail warden who transforms six deadly prisoners released on parole into persons of virtue and good morals. The film is based on Gandhian philosophy and raises the issue of prison reforms. It is based on a real life experience carried out by a prison reformer in a princely state during the British Raj. The film was widely acclaimed and exhibited at various International Film Festivals.

The movie had some highly effective performances by its cast. With all other technical excellences, it had a very popular music score as well. Its song '*Sainya jhooton ka bada sartaj nikla*' sung by Lata Mangeshkar, became highly popular. And its song '*Aye malik tere bandye hum, ayese ho hamaare karam*' is still recited in the prayer assemblies of many Indian schools.

Memorable songs of ' Do Aankhen Barah Haath'

Song	Singers
Sainya jhooton ka bada sartaj nikla	Lata Mangeshkar
Ho umad ghumad kar aaye re ghata	Lata Mangeshkar and Manna De
Main gaun tu chup ho jaa	Lata Mangeshkar
Aye malik tere bandye hum, ayese ho hamaare karam	Lata Mangeshkar
Tak Tak dhum dhum	Lata Mangeshkar and others

Story

The movie is set in a jail whose jailor is an idealist. He firmly believes in the goodness of human beings. This idealistic jail warden, Adinath (V.Shantaram) attempts to reform half a dozen die-hard criminals by conducting a unique experiment on them. The experiment involves letting them farm on a patch of land. Adinath argues that prisoners, even murderers, are human beings who can be redeemed if they are well treated. He takes six prisoners to his experimental barren farm, called Azad Nagar *(Freetown)*, where he demonstrates and helps them to reform into law-abiding citizens by giving them trust and respect.

He becomes their father figure or Babuji. His eyes *(Do Aankhen)* keep close watch on their twelve hands *(baarah haath)*. Sandhya (his real-life third wife) as the toy-seller provides light moments, though she is also the focus of discourses about sexuality and motherhood.

The convicts cultivate land and sell the produce in the markets at rates lower than the prevalent rates. The village landlord resents this and gets the convicts drunk and has them beaten to provoke them. However, Adinath's work shines through and none of them display any criminal tendencies despite provocation. The landlord, still angry, has Adinath attacked and gored to death by an angry bull at a time when the convicts are soon going to be set free. He succumbs to his injuries, losing his life but winning the goal he had aspired for. The convicts are set free. But they have come to be so much in love with Azad Nagar that now, when they have finally earned their freedom, they don't want to go anywhere else.

Remarks

- During the filming, V. Shantaram battled with a bull and lost his one eye during the stunt.
- The popular and memorable song *'Aye malik tere bandye hum'* became a morning prayer in many schools.
- This film was Shantaram's crowning glory. He played the character role as Adinath, a Jain name.

Awards

National Award

- President's Gold Medal (Best Film)
- President's Silver Medal

Other Awards

- Hollywood Press Association -- Samuel Goldwyn Award best foreign film
- VII International Film Festival at Berlin Silver Bear Award
- His Holiness the Pope's Catholic Award

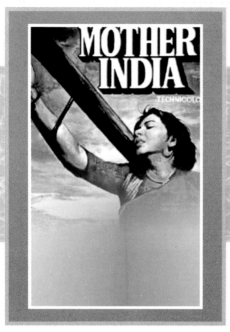

Mother India 1957

Director	Mehboob Khan
Producer	Mehboob Khan (Mehboob Productions Pvt.Ltd.)
Story & Screenplay	Mehboob Khan
Dialogues	S.Ali Raza and Wajahat Mirza
Starring	Nargis................as Radha
	Sunil Dutt.............as Birju
	Rajendra Kumar....as Ramu
	Raj kumar.......as Shamu, Radha's husband
	Kanhaiyalal....as Sukhilala the Moneylender
	Jilloo, Kumkum, Chanchal, Mukri, Azra,
	Sheela Naik, Sitara Devi
	Master Sajjid as young Birju
Music	Naushad
Lyrics	Shakeel Badayuni
Cinematography	Faredoon A. Irani
Sound	Kaushik
Editing	Shamsudin Kadri
Release date(s)	1957
Running time	172 min
Language	Hindi (Colour)

Mother India is an epic of rural India, weaving within its fold the very soul of Indian woman and her endurance and courage in the face of hardships and misfortunes. It is the

story of a helpless woman burdened down by poverty and subject to all exploitation, yet who unflinchingly braves it all without compromising on her culture and values upheld by love and devotion.

Mother India, a true classic, was a major box office hit. It was also the first Indian film ever to be nominated for the Academy Awards in the 'Best Foreign Language Film' category at the Oscars in 1958. At the screenings in Hollywood before the Academy Awards, the press hailed the memorable performances of Nargis and young Sajid. Eventually, though, *Mother India* lost by just one vote in the third poll and *Nights of Cabiria* won the award.

Besides a gripping and poignant story line, excellent screenplay and brilliant performances, one other thing that added to the success of *Mother India* was its remarkable music. It can be said that the film's music, like its story and characters, is bound to the soil. It has the fragrance of folk songs and the sweetness of rural simplicity and innocence. The songs range from the mischievous '*Ghoonghat nahi kholungi saiyan tore aage*', to deeply poignant numbers like '*Nagri nagri dware dware*' and '*Duniya mein hum aaye hain to jeena hi padega*'. But whether happy or sad, each and every song of this movie was a super hit and is still much loved by the lovers of Hindi film songs.

Memorable songs of 'Mother India'

Song	Singers
→ *Pee ke ghar aaj pyare dulhaniya chali*	Shamshad Begum and others
→ *Matwala jiya dole piya jhoome ghata chhaye re*	Lata Mangeshkar, Mohd. Rafi and others
→ *Umaria ghati jaye re*	Manna De
→ *Nagri nagri dware dware*	Lata Mangeshkar
→ *Duniya mein hum aaye hain to jeena hi padega*	Lata, Meena and Usha Mangeshkar
O janewale jaao na ghar apna chod kar	Lata Mangeshkar
Ghoonghat nahi kholungi saiyan tore aage	Lata Mangeshkar
Khat khut karti cham cham karti gaadi hamri jaye	Shamshad Begum, Mohd. Rafi and others
→ *Holi aaye re kanhaai rang barse*	Lata Mangeshkar , Shamshad Begum and others

The film begins with the finishing of a water canal at the village. Radha (Nargis), as the 'mother' of the village, is asked to inaugurate the canal. The event raises in her heart the memories of her past, and the film rolls into flashback..

She remembers the day when she was newly married. The wedding expenses between Radha (Nargis) and Shamu (Raj Kumar) were paid for by Radha's mother-in-law. She had mortgaged their land to the moneylender, Sukhilala (Kanhaiyalal) to raise this money. Radha comes to village to start her new life. She comes as the young bride with dream-laden eyes and quickly settles down to being a dutiful daughter-in-law and loving wife.

She is an ideal wife. She attends to the household and also works in the fields. Soon, the first child is born to her and brings the family great joy. On the other hand, the burden of debt upon them keeps on getting heavier and heavier and even fate seems to have turned agaisnt them. They are faced by mishap upon mishap. Their bullock dies and a new one can only be purchased with Radha's bridal ornaments. This event starts the spiral of poverty and hardships which Radha patiently and wordlessly endures. The conditions of the loan are disputed but the village elders decide in favour of the moneylender after which Shamu and Radha are forced to pay three quarters of their crop as interest on the loan of mere 500 rupees.

Whilst trying to bring more of their land into use to lessen the burden of their poverty, Shamu's both arms are crushed by a boulder. He is shamed by his helplessness and is humiliated by others in the village. He feels that he is of no use to his family so he decides to run away. He wakes in the middle of a night, wipes the 'Sindoor' from his sleeping wife's forehead (to symbolically indicate her widowhood) and leaves. Soon after this, Radha's mother-in-law dies as well. Radha is left alone with four children.

Radha continues to work in the fields with her children. Sukhilala offers to help alleviate her poverty in return for Radha marrying him, but she refuses to *sell herself*. Meanwhile, a storm sweeps through the

village, destroying the harvest and killing Radha's youngest child. The villagers start to migrate from the village but later decide to stay and rebuild their ruined lives on Radha.'s persuasion.

Radha, even after losing her husband, manages to survive through great toil, and raises her sons. When two of her children are dead and the remaining two starving for want of food, she goes to Sukhilala, prepared to sell her chastity in return for some rice. But at the last moment she finds new strength and fights back saying 'Sansar mein bas laaj hi naari ka dharm hai'.

Time passes and Radha grows old. Her two surviving children, Ramu (Rajinder Kumar) and Birju (Sunil Dutt), are young men. By now, she has become the respected and recognised leader of the village.

Her younger son Birju, embittered by the evils of Sukhilala since he was a child, takes out his frustration by pestering the village girls, especially Sukhilala's daughter. Ramu, by contrast, has a calmer temper and is married soon after. He becomes a father but his wife too gets absorbed into the cycle of poverty in the family. Birju's anger finally becomes dangerous and one day after being provoked, he attacks Sukhilala and his daughter, and also violently lashes out at his own family. On another occasion, as the village celebrates the festival of Holi, there is a violent showdown between Birju and Sukhilala. Birju is forced to flee the village, and turns into a dacoit in protest against the exploitation of the villagers and the sufferings of his mother. The moneylender becomes Birju's prime target.

On the day of the wedding of Sukhilala's daughter, Birju returns to take his revenge. He kills Sukhilala and abducts his daughter. But Radha promises to the village, to the soil and to the people of her rural community that Birju would not be allowed to sully the reputation and chastity of the young girl. To her, the village and her values are more important than the individual or the family. As Birju rides away with the girl, she shoots him down for the sake of the moral well-being of the village. Birju, her son, dies in her arms.

The film ends with her opening the gates of canal and water flowing into the fields. The water gushing out is reddish in colour- red not only with Birju's blood but the tears of blood that she has shed for him.

 **Remarks**

◑ *Mother India* was a remake of Mehboob Khan's own 1940 film- Aurat .

◑ The film resonates with high symbolism. While Radha and Shamu's marriage can be taken as mirroring the Independence of India and the beginning of a new life post-independence, Sukhilala, the moneylender, is symbolic of the brutal exploitation of poverty stricken Indian villagers. The troubles that Radha faces, her silent endurance, her sacrifices and her ultimate killing of her own son, all uphold the moral strength of Indian women.

◑ The character of Radha is, to this date, the most powerful role played by any actress ever on the Indian screen. After this movie, Nargis became a role model for successive generations of actresses.

◑ The film grossed over Rs.40 million. This record was beaten three years later by *Mughal-E-Azam* in 1960.

◑ Sajid, a pre-schooler, was chosen by legendary film producer/director, Mehboob Khan, for the role of the tough son, Birju (as a boy), from among hundreds of children.

◑ During the shooting of the film 'Mother India', on March 1, 1957 at 4.30 P.M. at Umra, the huge haystacks arranged in a circle for a scene suddenly caught fire. Nargis was surrounded by a wall of fire and the flames started to envelop her. Just in the nick of time, Sunil Dutt rushed in through the flaming haystacks and saved her. While coming out of the flames both of them got scorched. Some time after this incident, Sunil Dutt proposed to her. Later, they got married on March 11, 1958 at a quiet ceremony in Bombay.

◑ Rajendra Kumar, who plays Nargis's eldest son and Sunil Dutt's brother in the movie, also became a part of their family later on when his son Kumar Gaurav married Dutt and Nargis's daughter Anju (Namrata Dutt).

◑ The film was premiered on Friday. October 25, 1957 at Bombay's Liberty Cinema.

Awards

National Award

◔ Certificate of Merit (Now known as National Award)

Filmfare Awards

◔ Best Picture
◔ Best Director- Mehboob Khan
◔ Best Actress - Nargis
◔ Best Sound- Kaushik ◔ Best Cinematography- Faredoon Irani

International Award

◔ Karlovy Vary (Czechoslovakia)-1958 Best Actress Award Nargis for her stirring and persuasive performance.

PYAASA

Pyaasa **1957**

Director	❂	Guru Dutt
Producer	❂	Guru Dutt films Pvt Ltd.
Story	❂	Abrar Alvi and Guru Dutt
Script	❂	Abrar Alvi
Starring	❂	Mala Sinha ……………..as Meena
	❂	Guru Dutt ………………...as Vijay (Poet)
	❂	Waheeda Rehman…………as Gulab
	❂	Rehman………………….....as Ghosh
	❂	Johnny Walker……...........as Abdul Sattar
	❂	Kumkum, Shyam, Leela Misra
	❂	Mayadass,
	❂	Mehmood, Radhey Shyam
Music	❂	S.D.Burman
Lyrics	❂	Sahir Ludhianvi
Cinematography	❂	V.K.Murthy
Art Director	❂	Biren Naug
Editing	❂	Y.G.Chawhan
Dances	❂	Surya Kumar
Release date(s)	❂	February 22,1957
Running time	❂	146 min.
Language	❂	Hindi (B/W)

Pyaasa (English translation *Thirsty)*, directed by Guru Dutt, is saturated with the melodious melancholy of his tragic genius. It is a movie that can truly be described as a classic milestone in the history of Indian cinema. It's no surprise, therefore, that this film is rated as one of the best 100 films of all times by the Time magazine.

The film revolves around Vijay, a struggling poet trying to find recognition in post-independence India. At every step of his pursuit, he meets with deceit, selfishness and corruption that threaten to pull him down in the stifling confines of despondency. He is ultimately rescued by the love and devotion of Gulab, a prostitute with a heart of gold, who eventually helps him get his poems published.

This film is universaly recognised as one of the best works of Guru Dutt, alongside *Kaagaz Ke Phool* and *Sahib Bibi aur Ghulam*. It is, infact, the first directorial masterpiece by this genius storyteller and combines the efficacy of a poignant story, with brilliant direction, soulful music and songs that became instantly popular. The film not only *tells* the story of a poet struggling against a heartless materialistic world, it comes alive by the unique, memorable and powerful performance of all the actors in the film. The film, which Guru Dutt originally called 'Kashmakash', successfully reflects the relationship between a writer and his selfish publishers.

One of the highlights of this movie was its touching music and unforgettable songs. While some songs melted the heart with their romance, the others were either deeply poignant or hard hitting and biting satires on society. The song *'Malish, tel malish'* picturized on Johnny Walker was brilliantly humorous. These songs stirred the hearts of the masses at that time, and continue to do so till date.

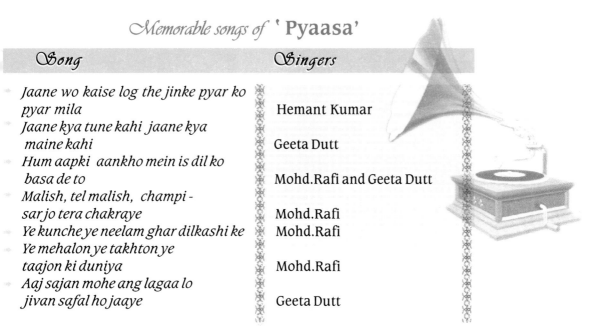

Memorable songs of ' **Pyaasa** '

Song	*Singers*
Jaane wo kaise log the jinke pyar ko pyar mila	Hemant Kumar
Jaane kya tune kahi jaane kya maine kahi	Geeta Dutt
Hum aapki aankho mein is dil ko basa de to	Mohd.Rafi and Geeta Dutt
Malish, tel malish, champi - sar jo tera chakraye	Mohd.Rafi
Ye kunche ye neelam ghar dilkashi ke	Mohd.Rafi
Ye mehalon ye takhton ye taajon ki duniya	Mohd.Rafi
Aaj sajan mohe ang lagaa lo jivan safal ho jaaye	Geeta Dutt

Pyaasa tells the story of Vijay, a poet, whose merit goes unrecognized by various publishers and who is deemed a failure by everyone, including his own brothers. The treatment that Vijay's poems get from the world is clearly brought out by the way Maulana, a newspaper editor, throws his poems into a waste paper basket. At home too, only his mother seems to acknowledge his poetic genius and believes in him. His own brothers, much to Vijay's surprise, humiliate him and sell his poems as scrap paper. He tries, but is unable to recover his work. One day, he hears his poetry being sung by a young prostitute named Gulab (Waheeda Rehman).

She lures him home, believing him to be a prospective customer but turns him out as soon as she finds he is penniless. As Vijay exits, he drops more of his work and Gulab realizes that she has shunned the very poet that she so loves. She is tormented by remorse and tries to make amends for his humiliation. She is the only person who appreciates his poetry and understands him. Friendship soon develops between them.

Besides Gulab, Vijay's only other friend is Abdul Sattar (Johnny Walker), a *telmalishwala*. He proves to be a good friend and together with Gulab he stays loyal to Vijay till the end.

Meanwhile, at a college reunion, Vijay comes across his former sweetheart Meena (Mala Sinha). She leads Vijay to believe that she is unmarried. But soon it is revealed that she is, in fact, married to Mr. Ghosh (Rehman), a prominent publisher. It doesn't take long for Vijay to realize that it was only his insecure financial condition that had prompted Meena to break her relationship with him. Ghosh, sensing a special relationship between Meena and Vijay, gives him a small job in his office. However, at a party at Ghosh's residence, Vijay finds himself being treated like a petty servant and feels deeply humiliated. And then, Meena even accuses him of re-entering her life and upsetting her settled family. Vijay is soon sacked from his job by Ghosh.

One day, while Gulab is in danger of being arrested by the police, Vijay saves her by calling her his wife. Her heart is touched by Vijay's act and she is filled with a longing to leave her bad life and set up a home. Soon after, Vijay's mother dies. The loss of his mother affects him such that he gives himself over to alcohol addiction. Feeling angry and depressed at the way things are going, he wanders over to the train yard. There, he donates his coat to a beggar.

The poor, homeless man is touched by Vijay's kindness and follows him. As fate would have it, he gets caught in the train tracks and is run over by a train. Since Vijay's coat is found on the

badly mutilated and unrecognizable body of the beggar, people think that it is Vijay himself who is dead. But in fact, Vijay was stunned by the sudden death of the man whom only a moment ago he had given his coat and some people take him to the hospital in a state of utter shock.

Gulab, grieving at Vijay's supposed death, spends all her money to publish his book of poems. This book of poems, called *Parchhaiyan* (Shadows), becomes an instant hit and enormously popular. Vijay's name becomes famous and he is finally accepted as a successful poet.

He himself, on the other hand, is still in the hospital. When he recovers, he tries to tell everyone that he is the real Vijay, the poet whom everyone is hailing as a genius now. But nobody believes him and even the doctor thinks that he has become deranged.In order to prevent the truth from coming out and to keep Vijay out of the way, Ghosh and Vijay's brothers conspire with the doctor and Vijay is thrown in a mental ward as a lunatic. He, however, manages to escape with the help of his old friend Abdul Sattar. When he reaches his home, his brothers (Mehmood and Mayadas) refuse to recognise him.

There is a public meeting being held to pay homage to him because the world thinks he is dead. Vijay goes there and emerges from the crowd to declare that he is the real Vijay. The audience, taking him to be a gatecrasher, beat him up for insulting the dead poet. His brothers, too, refuse to recognise him and deny the fact that the real Vijay is alive in lure of the money that is paid to them for lying.

But Maulana, the newspaper editor, with an eye on future profits, rescues him and announces that he is indeed Vijay. Ultimately, Vijay is verified to be himself.

By this time Vijay has become so disgusted at the corruption and selfishness of people around him that he denies he is the real Vijay at a second ceremony organised to honour his return. A riot erupts but Vijay, unperturbed by the public outcry, goes away. He goes to Gulab's house and asks her to come with him. She joins him without hesitation, and together, hand in hand, they walk away into the sunset

- *Pyaasa* was to be made with actresses, Nargis Dutt and Madhubala in the roles that Mala Sinha and Waheeda Rehman played eventually. But the two actresses couldn't decide which role they wanted to play and Guru Dutt eventually opted for Mala and Waheeda who were new in the film industry at that time.
- In keeping with the tradition of Guru Dutt films, comedian Johnny Walker had a hit song sequence, *Sar jo tera chakraye,* picturized on him.
- Initially Guru Dutt wanted to cast Dilip Kumar in the role of the poet.
- *Pyaasa* marked the last collaboration of the ever remembered team of S.D.Burman and Sahir Ludhianvi.
- Rehman's performance in both *Pyaasa* and *Sahib Bibi aur Ghulam* has been highly acclaimed.

KAAGAZ KE PHOOL

Kaagaz Ke Phool 1959

Director	Guru Dutt
Production	Guru Dutt Films Pvt.Ltd
Story	Abrar Alvi
Music	S.D.Burman
Starring	Waheeda Rehmaan …...as Shanti
	Guru Dutt ……………as Suresh Sinha
	Baby Naaz
	Mahmood, Mahesh Kaul, Minoo Mumtaz,
	Protima Devi,
	Johnny Walker, Veena, Nilofer, Mohan Choti,
	Tuntun, Shiela Vaz, Tony Waker.
Editing	Y.G.Chauhan
Cinematography	V.K.Murthy
Lyrics	Kaifi Azmi
Running time	148 min
Release date	2 October,1959
Language	Hindi (B/W)
Sound	S.V.Raman
Art	M.R.Achrekar

Kaagaz Ke Phool (English translation- *Paper Flowers*) was Guru Dutt's last movie as a director and one that is considered by many to be his finest film. This was the first Indian film made in wide 70 mm cinemascope.

It is the story of a creative spirit against the mindset that understands creativity only in terms of commercial success. The film is based on his own experiences with the actress, Waheeda Rehman, whom he launched and reportedly became emotionally involved with. It relates the poignant story of Suresh Sinha, a famous film director played by Guru Dutt himself. His marriage is on the rocks because of his wife's (Bina) elitist family, who consider filmmaking a disreputable profession. Suresh falls in love with

Shanti, played by Waheeda Rehman. He casts her in his movie, which makes her a famous actress. There are rumours of a romantic liaison between the two, but the romance is destined to be ill-fated. Although *Kaagaz Ke Phool* is much appreciated for its performances, songs, cinematography and directorial brilliance, it was however a commercial disaster when it was first released. It was a unique and experimental film based on a serious issue, but it did not find much favour with the masses. So much so, that Guru Dutt never officially directed a movie again. There is some speculation that *Sahib Bibi Aur Ghulam* was really directed by him, although it lists Abrar Alvi as the director. He, however, continued to produce films. The film's music was composed by S.D.Burman and the lyrics were written by Kaifi Azmi. '*Waqt ne kiya kya haseen situm*', sung by the director's wife Geeta Dutt, is the most famous song of the movie.

Memorable songs of 'Kaagaz Ke Phool'

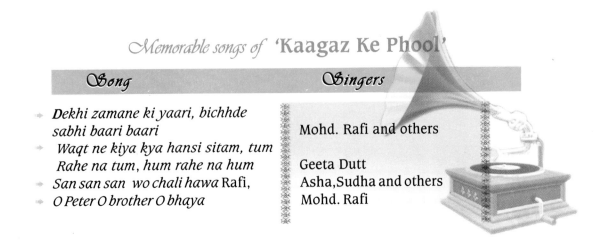

Song	Singers
→ *Dekhi zamane ki yaari, bichhde sabhi baari baari*	Mohd. Rafi and others
→ *Waqt ne kiya kya hansi sitam, tum Rahe na tum, hum rahe na hum*	Geeta Dutt
→ *San san san wo chali hawa* Rafi,	Asha,Sudha and others
→ *O Peter O brother O bhaya*	Mohd. Rafi

An old man enters a desolate film studio. He is Suresh Sinha (Guru Dutt), a former An old man enters a desolate film studio. He is Suresh Sinha (Guru Dutt), a former filmmaker. As he surveys the barren structures so familiar to him in his youth, the memories start swirling around him. Filmmaker. As he surveys the barren structures so familiar to him in his youth, the memories start swirling around him. He well Remembers how he had risen to fame as a successful filmmaker. He recollects when he made his film *Devdas* and had refused to take the popular actress Kanta, merely because she was unwilling to deglamourize herself for the role of the country girl, Paro.

Even though he had seen enormous success professionally, his marriage had been a failure. He was separated from his wife long ago and had been denied the permission even to meet his daughter. It was these disturbances in his relationships that had spilled over to the rising flame of his career and quenched it just when it was shining at its brightest.

One cold morning, Suresh meets Shanti (Waheeda Rehman), a sensitive orphan girl. She is shivering in the rain. Suresh gives her his coat and returns to Bombay.

The turning point in his life comes when he makes his film *Devdas* casting the unknown Shanti as Parvati against the protest of his producers. The film becomes a box offfice hit, and Shanti becomes the new sensation of the film world. The two gradually move closer to each other. Both now have a highly succesful career. But rumours about their friendship become public and reach Pammi, Suresh's daughter, who lives in a boarding school in Dehradun. She runs away from her school with a desire of somehow patch up the differences between her parents. Pammi comes to appeal to Shanti to stay out of her father's life and give her parent's marriage another chance. Pammi emotionally says to Shanti, *"You have no parents, but I do and am yet an orphan. I want to bring all of us together, but you won't allow it."* Moved by Pammi's plea, Shanti decides to leave films and throws it all up to go and teach in a village school.

Shanti's departure drives Suresh to alcohol. He loses all interest in his work and his career begins a downhill slide. His films begin to fail and his popularity is on the decline. He is sacked by his producer. Eventually, he gets a chance to make a comeback film only if it stars Shanti. She is willing but Suresh is not. He has lost everything but not his self respect.

His alcoholism keeps on getting worse. The court denies him the right to have any parental control over his daughter. Times passes and Suresh grows old. Meanwhile, Pammi has grown up and her marriage is fixed. Suresh has no money to give her a present. He returns to the film industry in search of some kind of employment. He gets a role as an *extra* but soon he flees from the studio when he finds that Shanti is the heroine of the film.

The story returns to the present, to the desolate studio and the old man watching his life go by. When the doors of the studio are thrown open later, and the crew returns, they discover his body- stilled in eternal rest in the director's chair.

Remarks

- Despite a grand premiere held in Delhi at the Regal Cinema, and attended by the then Vice President of India, Dr S.Radhakrishnan, the critics as well as the audience hastily rejected the film on its release. But today the film is termed as a classic and a milestone in the history of Indian Cinema.

Awards

Filmfare Awards

- Best Photography- V.K.Murthy
- Best Art direction - M.R.Achrekar

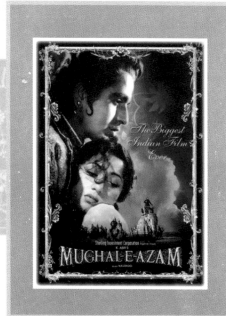

Mughal-e Azam **1960**

Producer	Sterling Investment Corporation
Director	K.Asif
Music	Naushad
Lyrics	Shakeel Badauni
Cinematography	R.D.Mathur
Starring	Prithviraj Kapoor
	Dilip Kumar
	Madhubala
	Durga Khote
	Nigar Sultana
	Ajit, Kumar
	Murad
	Jalal Agha, Vijayalaxmi,
	S.Nazir, Paul Sharma,
	Surendra, Johney Walker,
	Tabassum, Jillo Bai, Gopi
	Krishan.

Mughal-e-Azam is not just another movie, it's an epic saga of love that revolts against a monarch and forces him to bow his head. Produced and directed by K.Asif, it's a tale of royal romance, majestically told. Everything in this movie is large, regal and splendid, and yet, all too very human. Woven within the bejewelled fabric of this movie are emotions of a mother caught between a husband and a son, the dilemma of a father who has to uphold the sanctity of his royal throne even by sacrificing his son's heart, and the torment of a son who has to turn against his own father to win the right to love. And then, there's Anarkali, the lovely maiden who's hopelessly in love with a prince and knows that the turmoil that her innocent love has brought about can only terminate with the ending of her own life.

Mughal-e-Azam immortalized the Salim-Anarkali love legend, as well as each of its cast members and technicians. This grand magnum-opus was first launched in 1945 when the 'Quit India movement' was at its peak. However, it was soon stalled because some of the artists migrated to Pakistan after the partition. In 1950, it was started again with a new cast. Unfortunately, when ten reels of the movie had been shot, actor Chandramohan (who was acting as Akbar) suffered a fatal heart attack. He was replaced by Prithviraj Kapoor. Finally, after being in the making for fifteen long years, *Mughal-e-Azam* released on August 5, 1960 and became a milestone in the history of Indian Cinema. It became a super hit and held the record for the highest grossing film ever until the 1975 film *Sholay* broke its record.

The movie is special not just because of its grandeur and lavishness, but the super success that it earned can be attributed to many factors. It had a very beautiful love story, brought to life by powerful performances of Dilip Kumar as the dashing prince Salim, and the amazingly beautiful Madhubala as Anarkali. The intensity and passion of the star-crossed lovers, as well as their pain and sorrow is exquisitely brought out through several very romantic and beautifully picturised scenes. Who can forget the delicacy, romance and

sensuality of the scene where Salim caresses the downy cheek of Anarkali with a feather as moonlight bathes her ethereal beauty and a song *'Prem jogan ban jaoon'* plays in the background in Bade Ghulam Ali Khan's voice.

And adding magic to this romance was the exquisite cinematography and superb music and dance sequences. The songs of *Mughal-e-Azam* resound with the pride of love and echo with its pain as well. The song that Anarkali sings on the occasion of the Krishna Janmashtami, *'Mohe panghat pe nand lal ched gayo re'* was choreographed by none other than the famous Kathak maestro Lachchu

Maharaj. However, although all the songs of this movie touched the heights of popularity, the most loved song of this movie remains *'Jab pyar kiya to darna kya'*. It has actually acquired the status of a love anthem with every young heart throbbing in love repeating its lyrics to derive courage and inspiration.

Memorable songs of 'Mughal-e-Azam'

Song	Singers
Shub din aayo raj dulara and *Prem jogan ban ke sundri*	Bade Ghulam Ali Khan
Mohe panghat pe nand lal ched gayo rey	Lata Mangeshkar and others
Aye ishk ye sab duniya wale	Lata Mangeshkar
Mohabbar ki jhooti kahani pe roye	Lata Mangeshkar
Jab pyar kiya to darna kya	Lata Mangeshkar and others
Aye mohabbat zindabad zindabad	Mohd. Rafi and others
Ye dil ki lagi kam kya hogi	Lata Mangeshkar
Khuda negeh baan ho tumhara	Lata Mangeshkar

Story

The great Mughal Emperor Akbar (Prithviraj Kapoor) has everything a monarch can ask for- immense wealth, vast empire and trusted ministers. What he doesn't have is a child, who could be the heir to his throne after his death. He goes for a pilgrimage to the *dargah* of *Salim Chisti* at Ajmer and prays for a son. His wish is fulfilled and his wife, Rani Jodhabai (Durga Khote), gives birth to a boy. Akbar lavishes all his affection on him. However, as the boy grows up, Akbar feels that his affection and the pampering and luxuries of the palace are spoiling him. He sends prince Salim away to be brought up amid his soldiers so as to make him a brave warrior and a worthy prince.

When Salim grows up and returns to the kingdom, everyone is overjoyed. He has become a dashing and courageous prince who has earned much fame as a soldier. But despite being brought up as a warrior, he still has the heart of a romantic poet that loves beauty and appreciates music and art.

Love strikes when Salim unveils a statue. The statue is of a woman so beautiful that Salim instantly falls in love with it and wishes it were a real live girl of flesh and bones. As it is soon revealed, the statue is in reality a living girl made to stand still by the statue maker because the actual statue that he had promised to deliver hadn't been completed in time. This girl is a lovely courtesan whom Akbar gives the name of Anarkali.

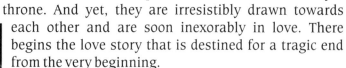

Salim and Anarkali fall in love with each other and soon follows a charming exchange of romantic letters. They both know that thei r love would not be accepted by the emperor. Anarkali (Madhubala) is just a dancing girl in the Mughal Court whereas Salim is a prince and the heir to the royal throne. And yet, they are irresistibly drawn towards each other and are soon inexorably in love. There begins the love story that is destined for a tragic end from the very beginning.

Emperor Akbar (Prithviraj Kapoor) forbids Salim to continue this affair. It leads to a struggle between the father and his adamant son as well as between public duty and personal desire. Salim leads a campaign against his father, is defeated and sentenced to death. Anarkali offers to sacrifice her life to save Salim and is to be buried alive, although Akbar allows her to escape through a secret tunnel unknown to Salim.

Remarks

● The film's most famous dance sequence takes place in the Sheesh Mahal (Palace of Mirrors), which was constructed at Mohan Studio with glass specially imported from Belgium. It was 30 feet high, 80 feet wide and 150 feet long. It took the workers from north India two years to build. In this Sheesh Mahal a defiant slave-girl (played by Madhubala) dances for the Mughal Emperor and his court, singing *Pyar kiya to darna kya*. This song was one of the three sequences shot on Eastman Kodak colour film, while the rest of the movie was in black and white. This set with its innovative use of mirrors, became a tourist delight. The Sheesh Mahal stayed put for two years after shooting had been completed and tourists had to remove their shoes before entering the mirrored palace.

● Once, a foreign unit researching Bollywood mistook Madhubala for a Venus statue. This incident gave her the title of 'Venus Beauty'.

● The film was shot in the desert of Rajasthan. Prithviraj Kapoor walked barefoot on the burning desert sand in torrid May upto Salim Chisti's *Dargah* in Ajmer for the scene that shows Akbar going to the *Dargah* to pray for a son. It was the most realistic shot of his life.

In 2004, a colorized version of the movie was released. The movie was again a success. After a gap of about forty years, the film was screened in colour in Pakistan for the first time in May, 2006.

The picturisation of the song '*Mohe panghat pe...*' took five days to choreograph. During each of those five days, a stranger was present on the set at Mohan Studio. He was the late Pakistani premier Zulfikar Ali Bhutto, who was staying at Worli, Bombay in those days.

About 20 songs were recorded for *Mughal-e-Azam* but out of them, ten songs, including '*Husn ki baraat chali*', sung by Shamshad Begum-Mubarak Begum and Lata Mangeshkar, were never heard by any one.

Awards

National Awards

- President's Silver Medal

 Filmfare Awards

- Best Film
- Best Cinematography
- Best Dialogue Writer

Sahib Bibi Aur Ghulam **1962**

Director	●	Abrar Alvi
Producer	●	Guru Dutt Films Pvt Ltd.
Story	●	Abrar Alvi
		Based on the novel by Bimal Mitra
Music	●	Hemant Kumar
Lyrics	●	Shakeel Badayuni
Starring	●	Meena Kumari
	●	Guru Dutt
	●	Rehman
	●	Harin Chatterji
	●	Waheeda Rehman
	●	Nazir Hussain
	●	Sapru, Sajjan, Dhumal, Mukund Banerji,
	●	Pratima Devi, Harin Chattopadhyaya.
Cinematography	●	V.K. Murthy
Editing	●	Y.G.Chauhan
Language	●	Hindi
Art direction	●	Biren Naug
Sound	●	P.Thackersey

Sahib Bibi Aur Ghulam is based on a Bengali novel of the same name written by Bimal Mitra, and is an insight into the tragic fall of the haveli-dom in Bengal during the British Raj. It tells the story of a young woman trapped within the suffocating confines of a feudal *Zamindar*

family. She yearns for the love of her husband who ignores her and prefers to spend time with prostitutes. There comes a time when she cannot bear it anymore and refuses to become just an adornment in the ancestral palatial mansion.

It was produced by Guru Dutt and directed by Abrar Alvi. The film's music is by Hemant Kumar. The film stars Guru Dutt, Rehman, Meena Kumari, Waheeda Rehman and Nazir Hussain, all of whom have given stellar performances.

The feel of a haunting melancholy running throughout the movie is further complemented by the superb melodies of: Hemant Kumar and the lyrics of Shakeel Badayuni. While on one hand the song *'No jao saiyaan chuda ke bahiyan'* expresses the yearning and sadness of *Chotti Bahhu* very beautifully, on the other *'Bhanwara bada nadan'* rings with the freshness and joy of a budding romance.

Memorable songs of 'Sahib Bibi Aur Ghulam'

Song

- *No jao saiyaan chuda ke bahiyan*
- *Sakiya aaj mujhe neend nahin aaye gi*
- *Bhanwara bada nadan*
- *Koi door se awaaz de chale aao*
- *Meri baat rahi mere man mein*

Story

Bhoothnath (Guru Dutt) is a middle-aged architect who is wandering through the ruins of an old *haveli*. With this scene, starts the flashback leading the audience back to the end of the 19th century.

The lower-class but educated Bhoothnath arrives in colonial Calcutta looking for work. He lives in the grand *haveli* of the Choudhurys, a family of *zamindars* while working beyond its compound at the Mohini Sindoor factory run by Subinay Babu (Nazir Hussain), a dedicated member of the *Brahmo Samaj*. Subinay Babu's young daughter Jabba (Waheeda Rehman) is amused by

Bhoothnath whom she considers an unsophisticated rustic. In the course of time, he develops an emotional tie with Jabba. He also becomes fascinated with  the happenings in the *haveli* and every night observes the decadent lifestyle of the Choudhury brothers. The men spend all their time living a life of pleasure. The women of the household have come to accept their subsidiary roles in the family through generations of suffering. The only exception is the childless *Chhoti Bahu* (Meena Kumari), wife of the impotent *Chhote Babu* (Rehman). She is a middle class girl who is brought into the family because of her great beauty. *Chhoti Bahu* cannot reconcile herself to the world of the Chaudhurys, where her husband spends his nights with prostitutes in the tradition of all aristocratic families. One night the servant, Bansi (Dhumal), takes Bhoothnath to meet the Chhote Babu's wife. She implores him to bring her 'Mohini Sindoor' (bridal vermilon) believing it will keep her unfaithful husband home. Bhoothnath is struck by her beauty and sadness and inadvertently becomes *Chhoti Bahu's* secret confidante.

A bomb explodes in the market place and Bhoothnath is injured in the ensuing crossfire between freedom fighters and British soldiers. Jabba looks after him with full devotion. After recovering, he becomes a trainee architect and goes away to work on a building project.

Chhoti Bahu repeatedly attempts to appease her husband but all her efforts fail till desperation makes her become his drinking companion in order to keep him by her side. Her husband ruthlessly taunts her about her orthodox ways. In retaliation, *Chhoti Bahu* takes to drinking and ultimately turns into an incurable alcoholic.

Bhoothnath returns some years later to Calcutta to find that Subinay Babu has died. He also comes to know that he and Jabba were betrothed as children. He returns to the *haveli* and is shocked to find it in partial ruin. *Chhoti Bahu* is now a desperate alcoholic and her husband is paralyzed. She asks Bhoothnath to accompany her to a nearby shrine to pray for her ailing husband. Their conversation is heard by the elder zamindar, *Majhle Babu* (Sapru). He orders his henchmen to punish her for consorting with a man outside the Choudhury household.
As Bhoothnath and Chhoti Bahu travel in the carriage, the carriage is stopped. Bhoothnath is knocked unconscious and *Chhoti Bahu* is abducted. When he wakes up in a hospital bed some days later, Bansi is by his side. Bhoothnath is told *Chhoti Bahu* has disappeared and the younger *zamindar* is dead. The truth is that she has already been killed and secretly

buried in the compound of the *haveli*. The flashback ends.

Bhootnath comes back to look at the ruins of the palatial *haveli* much later in his life. He has been happily married to Jaba for years. He recalls *Chhoti Bahu's* tragic history as he looks at the once splendid home, now silent and lifeless, a mute witness to a way of life that bore the seeds of destruction within itself. Meanwhile, Bhoothnath's workers inform him that a skeleton is found buried in the ruins of the *haveli*. From the jewellery on the corpse, Bhoothnath realizes it is the mortal remains of *Chhoti Bahu*.

Remarks

- ⊙ Meena Kumari'a performance as *Chhoti Bahu* is regarded as her best performance in Hindi films.
- ⊙ The famous song '*Na Jao Saiyaan*' by Geeta Dutt became a classic. Her voice, with all its sensuality and pain, complements Meena Kumari's performance perfectly.
- ⊙ This movie is re-made into a TV-series starring Raveena Tandon.
- ⊙ Nargis Dutt turned down the role of *Chhoti Bahu* to spend time with her infant son Sanjay. Initially, the role of Bhoothnath was offered to Shashi Kapoor and later Biswajit, too, was considered.
- ⊙ During the making of the film, Guru Dutt attempted suicide for the third time.

Awards

Filmfare Awards

- ◔ **Best Movie**
- ◔ **Best Actress** - Meena Kumari
- ◔ **Best Director** - Abrar Alvi
- ◔ **Best Cinematographer** - V.K. Murthy

National Award

- ◔ President's Silver Medal Award (1962), now known as National Awards.

Other Awards

- ◔ Bengal Film Journalists Association Award- Film of the year.
- ◔ The screening of the film provoked little reaction at the Berlin Film Festival
- ◔ It was nominated as an Indian entry for the Oscars.

Haqeeqat 1964

Producer and Director		Chetan Anand (Himalayan Films)
Story		Chetan Anand
Starring		Balraj Sahni, Dharmendra
		Priya Rajvansh, Jayant, Chand Usmani,
		Sulochna (Sr)
		Sanjay Khan, Vijay Anand, Sudhir,
		Bhupinder, Mac Mohan, Indrani Mukherjee
		Achala Sachdev, Shaukat Azmi
		Johnny Bakshi, Nasreen
Music		Madan Mohan
Lyrics		Kaifi Azmi
Cinematography		Sadanand Sengupta
Editing		M.D.Jadhav Rao
Release date(s)		1964
Running time		184 min.
Language		Hindi (B/W)

Haqeeqat was released in 1964, and ignited a sense of unity and patriotic pride among Indians at a time when national morale had hit rock bottom. *Haqeeqat* resulted in the resurgence of nationalist sentiment in the wake of the India-China War of 1962. This film deals honestly with the mistakes made by the leaders and the defeat suffered by India in the war. The film looks at the plight of those who mattered the most in the war - the *jawans,* and how they were betrayed by government policies that on one hand upheld the promise of peace and on the other, tied the hands of our armed forces and left them helpless in the face of merciless enemy.

The war had led to a sobering awareness of India's military capabilities. When China attacked India in 1962, our armed forces could have beaten them, but our foreign policy was such that they could not shoot without orders. The movie gave a very authentic portrayal of bravery, hardships and altruistic patriotism of our soldiers. It, however, had a very sad ending, quite like the result of the war on which it was based.

Haqeeqat to this date stands as one of the best Bollywood films based on war. The main strength of the film is its rugged landscape and authentic battle scenes that are seldom seen in Indian cinema. The movie was shot mostly on locations in the bleak non-judgmental landscape of Ladakh and the entire unit had to brave many climatic hardships.

The grim battle scenes aside, *Haqeeqat* is actually boosted by an extremely well written screenplay that engrosses the viewer. The audience is made to feel for even the smallest character and realize how a real soldier is forced to stay far away from his family and loved ones and fight for the country in sub-human conditions, facing death at every step.

This film is well supported by its large ensemble cast. As far as individual performances go, Balraj Sahni is his usual brilliant self as a Major in charge of the men. His feeling helpless at the situation and yet extolling his men to fight for the country is beautifully brought out. Jayant leaves his mark as well. Seasoned artists like Indrani Mukherjee, Achala Sachdev and Shaukat Azmi effortlessly do justice to their characters. This film was the debut film for Priya Rajvansh who played the role of Kammo, the love interest of Bahadur Singh (Dharmendra).

Another highlight of this movie is its unforgettable songs that resound with the zeal and vigour of a soldier's heart and are drenched with the pain and loneliness that these soldiers and their families have to face. The song '*Aayi ab ke saal diwali'* represents the loneliness of the beloved whose husband is away at war. The song *'Hoke majboor mujhe usne bulaya hoga'* sung by demoralized and exhausted soldiers emphasizes their plight and their longing for their wives and homes. And the heart-wrenching number, *'Kar chale hum fida jan-o-tan saathiyon'*, remains to this day, an unsurpassable salute to the altruism of martyrs that have been, and will be forever, the bastion of Indian independence.

Song	*Singers*
Zara si aahat hoti hai	Lata Mangeshkar
Masti mein chhed ke tarana	Mohd. Rafi
Main yeh sochkar uske dar se utha tha	Mohd. Rafi
Aayi ab ke saal diwali	Lata Mangeshkar
Hoke majboor mujhe usne bulaya hoga	Talat Mehmood, Mohd. Rafi and Bhupender
Kar chale hum fida jan-o-tan saathiyon	Mohd. Rafi and others
Khelo na mere dil se	Lata Mangeshkar

Story

The film's main plot revolves around a small platoon of Indian soldiers in the hilly terrain of Ladakh. Everybody considers these soldiers dead, but they are rescued by Kashmiri gypsies who also help the soldiers fight off the Chinese menace. They are asked to retreat from their post (*chowki*) as the Chinese forces surround them. Capt. Bahadur Singh (Dharmendra) and his gypsy girlfriend Kammo (Priya Rajvansh) die holding the Chinese at bay so that their comrades can
retreat to safety. But even the retreating soldiers are heavily outnumbered and give up their lives for the country.

Remarks

- Often in the film, the documentary footage is merged with fictional frames. In many scenes, art director M.S. Satyu blended the indoor sets of the Bombay studios with the outdoor locations of Ladakh. Of course, there are times the artificiality shows, but one is so swept away with the film that this technical flaw is overlooked.
- The film is brilliantly shot on locations, especially in case of the fiercely realistic battle scenes shot by cinematographer Sadanand Sengupta.

Awards

National Awards

- Certificate of Merit -Rs.10.000/- to the Producer and Rs.2,500/- to the Director

Sangam 1964

Director	◑	Raj Kapoor
Producer	◑	Raj Kapoor (R.K.Films)
Story	◑	Inder Raj Anand
Starring	◑	Raj Kapoor
	◑	Vyjayantimala
	◑	Rajendra Kumar
	◑	Lalita Pawar
	◑	Achla Sachdev
	◑	Iftekar
	◑	Nana Palsikar, Raj Mehra
Music	◑	Shankar-Jaikishan
Lyrics	◑	Shailendra, Hasrat Jaipuri
Cinematography	◑	Radhu Karmakar
Playback Singers	◑	Lata Mangeshkar, Mukesh,
	◑	Mohd. Rafi, Mahendra Kapoor
Editing	◑	Raj Kapoor
Art Direction	◑	M.R.Achrekar
Running time	◑	238 mins
Sound	◑	Allaudin
Language	◑	Hindi (Colour)

Sangam was Raj Kapoor's first color film which turned out to be a huge box office success. It was this movie that started the trend in Indian films of shooting song sequences abroad in *exotic* landscapes (particularly Switzerland). For the first time in Indian motion picture history, Raj Kapoor took an extremely top-heavy unit to shoot *Sangam* on foreign locations in Europe. The film was shot extensively in Venice, Paris, Switzerland, Rome and London. He made elaborate use of foreign locales for the honeymoon sequence in the film. It is no surprise, therefore, that *Sangam* got the highest ever collections from the overseas market (One hundred thousand pounds sterling).

Sangam was produced by R.K. Films and directed by Raj Kapoor. Initially, this film had been named as *Gharonda.* The film was distinguished by its technicolor photography and epic length. It was a big hit not only in India, but in South Asia, Middle East, Russia, Iran, Iraq and Egypt. *Sangam* once again proved to the world what a great artistic genius Raj Kapoor was and further strengthened his claim of being the biggest showman of Bollywood.

Its fabulous music was composed by Shankar-Jaikishan and the lyrics were penned by Hasrat Jaipuri. Like most other movies made by R.K. films, *Sangam* too is full of many remarkable songs. The songs range from naughty to romantic to deeply poignant. But they all have one quality in common, and that is melody.

Memorable songs of ' **Sangam** '

Song	Singers
Dost dost na raha	Mukesh
Har dil jo pyar karega	Mukesh, Lata and Mahender Kapoor
Main kya karun raam mujhe buddha mil gaya	Lata
Mere man ki ganga	Mukesh and Vyjayantimala
Mehbooba, o Mehbooba	Mukesh
O mere sanam, o mere sanam	Mukesh and Lata
Yeh mera prem patra padh kar	Mohd. Rafi

 **Story**

The movie stars Vyjayantimala, Raj Kapoor and Rajendra Kumar in a love triangle.

Sunder (Raj Kapoor), Gopal (Rajendra Kumar) and Radha (Vyjayantimala) are childhood friends. The film establishes clearly the economic and social disparity between Sunder and the other two. Sunder develops obsessive romantic feelings for Radha, but she prefers Gopal, who is also in love with her. Yet, as Sunder has confessed his feelings for Radha to him, Gopal decides to sacrifice his love for his friend.

Sunder asks Gopal to never let a man come between Radha and himself while he is away on his military mission. But when Sunder goes on this mission to Kashmir, he is shot down and is assumed dead. Grief brings Radha and Gopal closer and over time they confess their love for one another. But just when they are engaged to be married, Sunder suddenly returns. Gopal sacrifices his love again and Radha has no other choice but to marry Sunder.

They go on an extended honeymoon in Europe and seem happy enough with each other.

Radha is resolved to stay faithful to her husband and forget Gopal. But their married life is shattered when Sunder discovers an anonymous love letter to Radha. Sunder is thunderstruck. He bullies Radha to divulge the name of the suitor and threatens to kill the man, but she refuses. Sunder becomes obsessive with the letter and cannot return to normality.

Gopal finally confesses to Sunder in a dramatic scene that it was him who wrote the letter, and then commits suicide. Radha and Sunder are finally reunited in mourning.

Remarks

● Raj Kapoor had always been interested in making films that would appeal to the masses. Hence questions of popularity and box-office success were never far from his mind. His decision to shoot the film in exotic foreign locales was motivated by the commercial advanatges of treating the audience to something they had never before seen in Hindi films.

This love triangle is a psychologically multi-faceted tale about male bonding and the meaning of love and friendship. In the context of these relationships, Sunder is the one who is preventing the other two people's happiness and finally also thwarts his own. He appears as being naive and innocent, yet he is adamant at only noticing things that suit his own mindset. An important and critically regarded theme in the film is male bonding and the informal sharing of a woman between two male friends. Gopal indulges in his own sacrifice, but never thinks of the woman's feelings he ostensibly loves.

Awards

Filmfare Awards

- **Best Director**   Raj Kapoor
- **Best Actress**   Vyjayanthimala
- **Best Sound Recordist**   Allaudin
- **Best Editor**   RajKapoor

Other Awards

Association of Film Editors, Bombay

- Certificate of Merit awarded to Raj Kapoor. *Sangam* adjudged the Best Edited Film of the year-1964. Certificate presented by Hrishikesh Mukherjee

The Bengal Film Journalists Association

- Certificate of Merit awarded to R.K.Films. *Sangam* adjudged by the BFJA as among the 10 Best Films of 1964

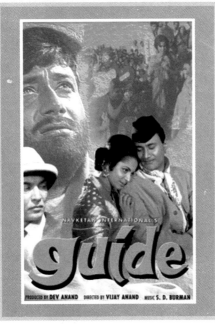

Guide 1965

Director		Vijay Anand (Goldie)
Producer		Vijay Anand (Navketan International)
Story		Vijay Anand
		Based on the novel by R.K.Narayan
Starring		Dev Anand ....Raju
		Waheeda Rehman ... Rosie
		Leela Chitnis ....Raju's Mother
		Kishore Sahu ....Marco
		Jagirdar, Anwar, Ulhas, Purnima
		Krishan Dhawan
Music		S.D.Burman
Cinematography		Fali Mistry
Editing		Vijay Anand
		Babu Sheikh
Release date(s)		9 February 1965
Running time		183 min.
Language		Hindi (Colour)

Guide an Indo-American co-production, was a Hindi-English bilingual film directed by Vijay Anand, who also contributed with the screenplay. The movie is based on the critically acclaimed English novel by R.K.Narayan. The novel itself won a national literary prize. It is not surprising therefore, that the movie that was based upon the novel is also considered to be one of the masterpieces of Indian film industry.

Guide was highly successful upon release and went on to earn the status of a classic, thanks to its thought provoking story, spell binding performances and popular song tracks. It had a unique plot that inspired highly effective performances from the lead actors. Waheeda Rehman herself has said that Rosie was the best role she played, and most critics consider Dev Anand's performance as Raju guide in this movie to be his finest.

All the songs of this movie became very popular and are considered classics in their own rights.

Memorable songs of 'Guide'

Song	Singers
Kaanton se khinch ke ye aanchal	Lata
Gaata rahe mere dil	Lata and Kishore
Piya tose naina laage re	Lata
Wahaan kaun hai tera	S.D.Burman
Allah megh de	S.D.Burman
Tere mere sapne ab ek rang hai	Mohd. Rafi
Din dhal jaye haaye raat na jaaye	Mohd. Rafi
Kya se kya ho gaya	Mohd. Rafi

Story

The movie starts with Dev Anand coming out of jail, and then the story runs in flashback. Dev Anand stars as Raju, a freelance guide in Rajasthan, who earns his living by taking visitors to historic sites. One day, a wealthy and elderly archaeologist Marco (Kishore Sahu) comes to the city with his young wife Rosie (Waheeda Rehman). Marco and Rosie disembark at the station and bump into Raju. Marco wants to do some research on the caves outside the city and hires Raju as his guide. It doesn't take too long for Raju to realize that their marital life is on the rocks. Raju develops a soft corner for

Rosie. He comes to learn about Rosie's past and her love for dancing, which is something totally unacceptable to Marco.

Marco gets busy with the caves and Raju takes Rosie out for a tour of the nearby sites. On returning back to Udaipur, Rosie discovers that Marco is more interested in sculptures and prostitutes than his wife. She also discovers that he's having an affair with a native tribal girl. Raju gives Rosy the love and sympathy that she craves for from her unsympathetic and insensitive husband. He induces her to leave Marco and come with him, and she does exactly that. She feels so liberated after leaving her husband that she is shown actually celebrating her break-up. This is perhaps the only time in a Hindi film where a wife is shown singing a happy song *(Aaj phir jeene ki tamanna hai)* on leaving her husband.

Raju appreciates her dancing skills and promises her fame and fortune, if only she would do as he says. He lures her away and they start living together. She remains married to Marco despite living with Raju. After learning of Raju's affair with Rosie, his mother (Leela Chitnis) leaves him. His friend and driver also abuse him and severe all ties with him. He loses his business and the entire town develops animosity towards him.

Undeterred by these setbacks, Raju helps Rosie embark on a singing and dancing career, and she achieves instant stardom. As Rosy becomes famous, thanks to her superb dancing skills, Raju uses her to satiate his passion for money With money in hand, Raju falls into bad habits, and takes to gambling and drinking. One day, he is caught forging a cheque with Rosie's signatures. He is arrested and lands up in jail as a criminal. On the day of his release, his mother and Rosie come to pick him up but they are told that he was released six months earlier because of his good behaviour.

Upon his release Raju wanders alone and comes to a village. A farmer (Bhola) finds him sitting alone in a temple and mistakes him for a saint. Bhola is having a problem with his sister, Raju uses his vocal skills and practical knowledge to convince the girl to act according to her brother's wish. Impressed by this, Bhola spreads the news through the village, and Raju is taken as a holy man by the uneducated and simple village people. The villagers start bringing gifts for him and seeking his advice for solving all their problems. Initially, Raju enjoys this newly endowed demi-god status, as this provides him with food, shelter and all the basic necessities without working too hard. He makes the village temple his abode and starts acting like a real saint. He even grows a beard and starts dressing like a holy hermit as well. People start calling him Swami Raju. Slowly, he learns of the problems that plague the life of his disciples, and actually starts taking interest in their lives. He acts as a teacher to the village kids, and makes efforts to make the life a better experience for his followers.

A famine hits the whole region and the villagers begin fearing for the worst. They ask their spiritual guru (Raju) to go on a fast to bring rain. At first Raju opposes the idea, going as far as telling Bhola that he is just an ordinary human being like all of them and even worse, a convict. But even the confession is not enough for the villagers to give up on their belief. He reluctantly goes on a fast, although he does not believe that there is any relation between a man's hunger and rain. As hunger and resolution wage a battle for supremacy over him, Raju undergoes a spiritual transformation. As the duration of his fast increases, his fame starts spreading and people from all corners come to see him and take his blessings. He is transformed into a saint, the saviour of a drought-stricken village.

In one of the most memorable scenes, an American journalist asks him whether he truly believes that his fast would bring rain, he smiles and says *"These people have faith in me, and I have faith in their faith"*.

Upon hearing his fame, Rosie pays him a visit. His mother and his friend arrive too. He now has everything that he had lost a long time back. In the final scenes of the movie, with his strength failing and physical condition getting serious, he starts thinking about the meaning and purpose of his life. He has two options before him. On one hand, he has the option to escape, go back to his past life and live with Rosie and his mother. On the other hand, there is the cause that he, although unwillingly, has adopted. He eventually decides not to end his fast.

In the final scene, when it starts raining and everyone rushes outside, he's left behind. He is now all alone in the house of God, his heart cleansed of all ills, and soul ready to fly up to the purest heights. He hears the sound of raindrops and collapses.

Remarks

●   Initially, even Goldie advised his big brother Dev Anand against making this film. He said that it was a wrong theme for an international project. He was horrified when he went through the screenplay of the English version. It was not good and would have ruined the image of the country. The English version of *'Guide'* was a disaster at the box office. Not even the much hyped nude scene (with duplicate) could save the film. With the disaster of the English version, no distributor was interested in buying the Hindi version. But the veteran producer Yash Johar decided to take matters into his hands. It was only because of him that the movie finally released. Its premiere was held at Bombay's Maratha Mandir in 1965. Though the initial response was lukewarm, the film enjoyed a house-full run for 10 weeks thereafter.

Anand 1970

Director	●	Hrishikesh Mukherjee
Producer	●	Hrishikesh Mukherjee
	●	N.C.Sippy
	●	Romu N. Sippy
Story	●	Bimal Dutta,
	●	Gulzar, D.N.Mukherjee,
	●	Hrishikesh Mukherjee
Starring	●	Rajesh Khanna .... as Anand Saigal
	●	Amitabh Bachchan .....as Dr. Bhaskar Banerjee
	●	Sumita Sanyal........... as Renu
	●	Ramesh Deo, Seema Deo, Johnny Walker,
	●	Lalita Pawar, Dara Singh,
	●	Durga Khote and Asit Sen
Music	●	Salil Chaudhary
Dialogue and Lyrics	●	Gulzar and Yogesh
Release date(s)	●	1970
Running time	●	122 mins
Language	●	Hindi (Colour)

Anand is considered as one of the greatest Hindi movies of all times. It beautifully captures one of the greatest philosophies of life through the character of an exuberant young man who loves life and lives it to its fullest even though he knows that he does not have much of it left in his grasp. Anand, the protagonist, sums up the philosophy in one

line *'Zindagi bari honi chahiye, lambi nahin',* meaning that life should be vivacious and magnanimous, not necessarily long. It is not just a movie that tells of a man dying of cancer, but presents before our eyes a drama of mortality that Hrishikesh Mukherjee moulded into an immortal affirmation of life.

It was written and directed by Hrishikesh Mukherjee and starred Amitabh Bachchan and Rajesh Khanna in what is to this time one of their most memorable roles. The film was both a critical and commercial success. The dialogues as well as the lyrics for the film were written by the acclaimed poet and writer Gulzar. The musical score was written by Salil Chaudhary.

The songs of this movie are so marvellously penned that they are poignant yet not sad, philosophical without being boring and dull, and so melodious and tuneful that they remain the favourite of many even to this day. The song *'Zindagi kaisi hai paheli haye, kabhi hansaye kabhi rulaye'* is an absolute philosophical masterpiece.

Memorable songs of **'Anand'**

Song	*Singers*
Maine tere liye hi saat rang ke sapne chune	Mukesh
Na jiya jaye na	Lata
Maut tu ek kavita hai	Poem
Kahin door jab din dhal jaaye	Mukesh
Zindagi kaisi hai paheli haye, kabhi hansaye kabhi rulaye	Manna De

Dr Bhaskar Banerjee (Amitabh Bachchan) wins a prize for a book titled *Anand*, which relates his experience with a cancer patient Anand Saigal. As he starts speaking about his book, the story unfolds in flashback.

The film is about Anand Saigal (Rajesh Khanna), a cancer patient who wants to enjoy every minute of life, whatever little of it is still left with him. He is a young man who, despite knowing fully well that he is dying, believes in living his life to the fullest. On the other hand, Bhaskar Banerjee is a sober doctor, upset with life and the dark realities of corruption and deceitfulness pervading the society. He sees the ills blighting the country and knows that none of this is going to get any better. He is angry at the state of society,

disapproves with his friends for not minding the ills around them, and is annoyed with himself as well for being a part of such a system.

When he comes across Anand, he finds in him a person who is speeding towards an untimely death and yet has his eyes focussed on the vibrant hues of the world around him. To him the world is still a beautiful place full of love and goodness. As Anand and Bhaskar come closer and become friends, Bhaskar too begins to see the world the way Anand

sees it and notices the colours of life behind all those despairs and complexities that surround it.

Anand is the kind of person who likes to bring up a smile on every face around him. His playful and happy ways endear him to one and all. However, soon that moment comes when his time runs out. After spreading happiness around himself and changing the lives of many, he succumbs to his disease. In the end, all that is left is the love that he helped to

bring in the lives of his friends and the memories that inspire Bhaskar to write a book on his life and share with the world the way of living that Anand had taught him.

Remarks

◉ *Anand* was remade in Malayalam, with the name *Chitrashalabham* (butterfly) starring Jayaram and Biju Mohan.

◉ The movie was inspired with and dedicated to Raj Kapoor who used to call Hrishikesh Mukherjee *Babu Moshai*. He wrote the film *Anand* initially with Raj Kapoor in mind. The two shared a great deal of affection.

◉ There is a dialogue in the film where Rajesh Khanna says '*Jeena Bombay mein, marna Bombay mein*'. This was inspired from the famous Raj Kapoor dialogue '*Jeena yahan marna yahan*'.

◉ Hrishikesh Mukherjee initially offered the role of Anand Saigal to Kishore Kumar, Shashi Kapoor and even to Raj Kapoor, but finally decided on Rajesh Khanna.

◉ Hrishikesh Mukherjee penned the story of *Anand* in 1954. The idea of this film was borrowed during Berlin Film Festival from a Japanese Film *Ikiru* about a man with cancer who has just six months to live.

Awards

National Awards

- Best Regional Film in Hindi.
- Rs.5000/- to the Producers and Silver Medal to the Director

Filmfare Awards

- Best actor (Rajesh Khanna)
- Best dialogue (Gulzar)
- Best editor (Hrishikesh Mukherjee)
- Best film (Hrishikesh Mukherjee, N.C. Sippy)
- Best story (Hrishikesh Mukherjee)
- Best supporting actor (Amitabh Bachchan)

Mera Naam Joker **1970**

Director	●	Raj Kapoor
Producer	●	Raj Kapoor (R.K.Films)
Story, screenplay and dialogue	●	K.A.Abbas
Starring	●	Raj Kapoor as Raju (The Joker)
	●	Simi Garewal......as Mary
	●	Manoj Kumar......as David
	●	Rishi Kapoor.......as Young Raju
	●	Dharmendra.......as Mahendra
	●	Dara Singh.........as Sher Singh
	●	Ksiena Ryabinkina.. as Marina
	●	Padmini.............as Meena,
	●	Rajendra Kumar, Rajendra Nath,
	●	OmPrakash, Agha, Achla Sachdev
Music	●	Shankar-Jaikishan
Lyrics	●	Shailendra, Hasrat Jaipuri, Neeraj, Prem
	●	Dhawan and Shaily Shailendra
Cinematography	●	Radhu Karmakar
Playback Singers	●	Mukesh, Asha Bhonsle, Mohd.Rafi
	●	Manna De, Master Nitin
Editing	●	Raj Kapoor
Art Direction	●	M.R. Achrekar
Distributed by	●	R.K.Films

Sound	❍	Allaudin
Release date	❍	8th December,1970
Country	❍	India
Language	❍	Hindi/English/Russian (Colour)

Mera Naam Joker (English translation *My Name is Joker*) was another outstanding film made by the great showman Raj Kapoor. It revolves around a clown who must make his audience laugh even if his own heart is full of sorrow. It was reportedly inspired by Raj Kapoor's own life and the clown is said to be an allegory for his life as an actor.

The screenplay for this movie was written by Khwaja Ahmad Abbas. Rishi Kapoor, Raj Kapoor's second son, made his debut in this film as a child artist.

Mera Naam Joker is adorned with several melodious songs. Music has always been a strong point of all R.K. Films, and *Mera Naam Joker* is no exception. Every song of this movie is a feat in itself and finds a place in the list of all time favourites.

Memorable songs of 'Mera Naam Joker'

Song	Singers
➜ *Kahta hai joker sara zamana*	Mukesh
➜ *Jaane kahan gaye wo din*	Mukesh
➜ *Jeena yahan marna yahan, iske siva jaana kahan*	Mukesh
➜ *Teetar ke do aage teetar*	Mukesh, Asha Bhosle and Simmi
➜ *Aye bhai zara dekh ke chalo*	Mukesh
➜ *Daag na lag jaayye*	Manna De

The film revolves around the life of Raju (Raj Kapoor), who chooses to become a clown so that he could make people laugh. It traces Raju's journey from his childhood to the day of his last performance.

The film begins with a circus having come to town and announcing a surprise programme: the last performance of the famous clown Raju. Three women are special invitees- Mary, a teacher, Marina, a beautiful Russian dancer and Mina, a film star. In the ring, Raju stages his act. He is a clown who is sick, while the other clowns, as doctors and surgeons operate upon him and take out his 'enlarged' heart. One of the clown doctors, while handing the heart to Raju, says *"Keep it safe. It is getting bigger all the time. One day the whole world will be accommodated in your heart'"*. This makes the clown very happy. He sings *'Jina yahan marna yahan, iske siva jana kahan..'* and dances with his heart, throwing it up in the air. It comes down and shatters into a thousand pieces. From here on, the film, structured in three chapters, recounts the story of Raju and the women in his life.

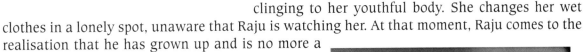

Raju's father, also a clown, had been considered the best circus clown of his time. However, ever since he met with an untimely death in a trapeze accident during his performance, Raju's mother has started hating the very name of circus. She wants Raju to study in a good school so that he could do well in life. As luck would have it, Raju has a natural affinity towards the circus and a desire in his heart to make people laugh.

Mera Naam Joker is divided into 3 chapters. The first chapter is about the adolescent Raju. He is infatuated with his beautiful young teacher, Mary (Simi Garewal) who is many years older than him. One day Raju, hiding in the bushes, sees Mary fall into the river. When she comes out of the water, her clothes are clinging to her youthful body. She changes her wet clothes in a lonely spot, unaware that Raju is watching her. At that moment, Raju comes to the realisation that he has grown up and is no more a little child. When Mary goes on a holiday, he gives her a doll which looks like a clown. He feels that like a clown, he too is born to make the world laugh, even through his own troubles. When Mary comes back after holidays, she is engaged with David (Manoj Kumar). Soon after, Raju is sent away from the school for clowning in the streets to earn money for the treatment of his sick mother. He is invited as a best man in the wedding of Mary, where her husband David gives him back the doll saying that one day he will grow old but the doll will always remain young.

After his first heartbreak, the story moves on

to the adult Raju who is working with Gemini Circus. A group of Soviet artistes arrive to perform with the circus. After going through many misadventures, he establishes his place in the circus as a singing clown. The circus is owned by Mahendra (Dharmendra). Here, he meets Marina (Bolshoi Ballerina Kseina Rabinkina), a Russian trapeze artist. And although there is a language barrier between them, he falls in love with her and dreams of a married life with her. He gifts her the same clown doll that he had gifted to Mary. But Raju is heart broken once again when Marina returns to Russia to her aged and ailing father. The

doll he had gifted to her is once again handed back to him. It is in this chapter that Raju's mother dies a tragic death just before Raju's performance. But since *the show must go on*, he has to go up on the stage regardless of his personal tragedy and make the audience laugh.

Dejected and heartbroken, he soon leaves the circus. Being tired with the repeated return of the doll, he throws it away into the sea. But a dog picks it up and brings it back to him. The dog belongs to a boy, Meenu, who is pasting film posters on billboards near the beach. Meenu, Moti (the dog), and Raju start a travelling circus of their own. One day, Raju discovers that Meenu is actually a girl and not a boy. She tells him that she deliberately remains in disguise to protect herself. She has an ambition of becoming a famous actress. Raju doesn't want to risk falling in love again and wants to go away from Meena. She, however, manages to overcome Raju's hesitation and makes him stay on with her. Soon they come closer and Raju once again loses his heart to this beautiful girl. In the meantime, she meets a famous young actor Kumar

(Rajendra Kumar). Kumar, who is also a producer, introduces Meena on the silver screen as a new actress. Soon she becomes a successful and glamorous star. Now, she has no need for Raju's support. He realizes that there is no longer any place for him in her life. She's happy with her new found fame and the glittering world of glamour. Kumar tells him that by staying on with Meena, he is only fettering her eager wings. So he makes his exit, leaving her free to fly away to success and fame.

In the end, Raju performs his last act in the presence of the three women whom he ad loved and lost. He picks up the broken pieces of his heart and announces that his story has ot ended at all and that the show will go on.

Remarks

- Raju always carries a clown doll which belonged to his father. Every time he falls in love, e gifts his beloved doll symbolising his heart, only to see it come back to him. Raj Kapoor has rilliantly portrayed the doll as a metaphor for Raju's simplistic heart where there is room for veryone.
- Six years in the making, with Raj Kapoor investing much of his own personal fortune, *Mera Naam Joker* was a huge commercial disaster. It fell face down at the box office, leading Raj apoor to the very tail-end of his resources. He reached the verge of bankruptcy, but dedication nd strong will-power helped him pull through. It was only much later that *Mera Naam Joker* vas acknowledged a masterpiece of directorial brilliance.
- Never before had any producer in the Indian film industry ever *imported* such a big group f foreign artists (Russian) to work in an Indian film (1967-68).
- The movie that was one of the biggest flops of 1970, become eighteen years later the hit f 1988. Today, this is one of the most popular films on the Indian video circuit. Even in the eventies, *Mera Naam Joker* created box office history outside India, finding much favour in atin America, Peru, Brazil, and Argentina. The Soviet Union, too, purchased it for their highest rice ever (Rs.15 Lakhs).
- Many different cuts of the film are known to exist. The IMDb cites 224 minutes, while ccording to the Chicago Reader, the original running time was 5 hours. Many prints run just ver 3 hours. The DVD release from Yash Raj films runs 3 hours, 44 minutes.

Awards

Filmfare Awards

- Best Director- Raj Kapoor,
- Best Music- Shankar Jaikishan,
- Best Cinematography- Radhu Karmakar
- Best Sound Recordist- Allaudin
- Best Playback Singer (Male) - Manna De

National Awards

- 'A plaque' for Best Child Actor below 16 years Rishi Kapoor
- Best Male Playback Singer
- Best Cinematography (Colour).

Pakeezah 1971

Director	●	Kamal Amrohi
Producer	●	Kamal Amrohi (Mahal Pictures Pvt. Ltd.)
Story, Screenplay,		
Set Design and Costume	●	Kamal Amrohi
Starring	●	Meena Kumari
	●	Raaj Kumar
	●	Ashok Kumar
	●	Veena, Nadira, Sapru, Kamal Kapoor,
	●	Vijaylaxmi, Jagdish Kanwal, Pratima Devi,
	●	Meenakshi, Zebunissa,
	●	Chandermohan
	●	Sarita Devi, S.Nazir, Rafia Sultan
Cinematography	●	V.K.Murthy
Lyrics	●	Majrooh Sultanpuri, Kaifi Azmi,
	●	Kamal Amrohi
	●	Kaif Bhopali
Music	●	Ghulam Mohammed
	●	Naushad
Singers	●	Mohd.Rafi, Lata Mangeshkar,
	●	Parveen Sultana, Vaani Jairam
Language	●	Hindi/Urdu (Colour)
Release dates(s)	●	1971

Pakeezah, an Urdu film released in 1971, was the magnum opus of the perfectionist director, Kamal Amrohi. It is magnificent in terms of its touching story of courtesan love, its tuneful songs, and the splendour of its chandelier-heavy, fountain-adorned Gulabi Mahal draped with flimsy curtains and inhabited by statuesque women with trailing *dupattas* and charming grace.

Added to this splendour is the exquisite poetic quality of this film. There's poetry in not just the diction of the characters and the picturisation of the scenes, but also in the marked symbolism of several visuals and sounds repeated throughout the movie. Only Kamal Amrohi, a director who was a poet as well, could have portrayed something as mundane as a train whistle into a thing of such beautiful poignancy.

The whole film has an aura of lavishness and grandeur that becomes apparent in not just the luxurious sets but also in the very personas of the characters that enliven this movie.

Not surprisingly therefore, that the movie took its own grand time of nearly fourteen years to be completed. And during these fourteen years, the relationship between Meena Kumari and the director, who was also her husband, changed considerably. Their warm and loving relationship experienced a lot of love loss and grew worse with time. Fortunately, none of this was allowed to cast any unwelcome reflection over the movie, which, when finished, proved to be a grand cavalcade of visual splendour, stringing within it a majestic saga of love, hope and despair.

In fact, Meena Kumari, the heroine of the movie, gave probably the best performance of her career for this movie. It was also her last performance. She died within two months of the film's release on 31st March, 1972 at the age of 40 years. When initially released, the film opened to a lukewarm response, and was expected to be a flop. However, Meena Kumari's untimely death made the public flock towards the theatre to catch the last performance of this very popular actress.

What added to the magic of this movie was its mesmerizing music and unforgettable songs. The *Mujras* of this movie, with the sounds of *ghungroos* echoing with the beat and the forlorn sound of the train whistle shrieking into the night, coupled as they were with Meena Kumari's expressive graces and brilliant dance performances, have become just as eternal in the annals of Bollywood history as the movie itself is.

Memorable songs of 'Pakeezah'

Song	Singers
Chalte-chalte youn hi koi mil gaya tha	Lata Mangeshkar
Thade rahiyo o banke yaar	Lata Mangeshkar
Inhi logon ne, le leena duppata mera	Lata Mangeshkar
Mausam hai ashiqana	Lata Mangeshka r
Chalo dildar chalo	Lata Mangeshkar and Mohd.Rafi
Teer-e-nazar dekhenge	Lata Mangeshkar
Kaun gali gayo shyam	Parveen Sultana
Mora saajan sautan ghar jaaye	Vani Jairam

Story

Shahabuddin (Ashok Kumar) is in love with a courtesan, Nargis (Meena Kumari) but his family will not let him marry her. The blonde-haired Nargis, seeks to escape her *kotha* [brothel] by eloping with her lover Shahabuddin. The patriarch of Shahabuddin's family refuses to accept her and feeling disgraced and dejected, she flees to a graveyard. It's in this graveyard that she gives birth to a daughter and dies. While on her deathbed, she writes Shahabuddin a letter asking him to come for his newborn daughter.

Her sister (Veena), who is also a courtesan, arrives first and finding Nargis dead, takes away the newborn child back to the *kotha*. This little unfortunate girl is brought up by her aunt (Veena) and becomes a popular courtesan herself when she grows up. The role of this girl, Sahibjaan, is played by Meena Kumari again.

The letter that Nargis had written to Shahabuddin, reaches him after several long years. Everything belonging to Nargis had been sold off soon after her death and the letter had remained trapped within a book for several years, till it was discovered by a book lover and finally forwarded by him to its destination.

Shahabuddin, after getting the letter, comes seeking his now adult daughter, Sahibjaan (Meena Kumari). But Sahibjaan's furious aunt takes her niece away and flees by train.

On the train journey, a dashing young man Salim (Raaj Kumar) enters the sleeping Sahibjaan's compartment and, enchanted by her feet, leaves behind a note that says, '*Aap ke paon dekhe, bahut haseen hai. Inhe zameen par mat utariyega, maile ho jayenge.*' (saw your feet, they are very beautiful. Do not let them touch the floor, otherwise they would get dirty). Ironically, as a courtesan, Sahibjaan necessarily has to put the same feet on the floor and figuratively dirty them by dancing the *mujra* to please her audience. The note gives Sahibjaan hope, even as she avoids unwelcome attention from her patrons.

The bird with clipped wings and the snake in the *kotha* serve as external symbols of the struggles in Sahibjaan's life. When she returns to her *kotha,* she's compared to a torn kite whose heart wants to fly away into freedom and who finds herself tied and tangled up to a rotting tree. In the film, two sound motifs throughout the film were effectively used --- the train's piercing whistle, which reminds Sahibjaan of her admirer and hope; and a soulful *alaap* by Lata Mangeshkar, which mirrors her moments of sadness.

Sahibjaan does meet Salim, but feigns amnesia to avoid telling him her reality. She is brought back to the *kotha*, but soon manages to run away and, coincidentally, bumps into

Salim again. She falls in love with him. Salim is a forest officer and as is soon revealed, is Shahabuddin's nephew.

Salim takes her home but the feisty patriarch will have none of it. Sahibjaan seems fated to re-live her mother's sad story. But Salim defiantly leaves home with her and when Sahibjaan confesses she is a *tawaif* (prostitute), steadfastly stands by her side. At their marriage, he refers to her as *Pakeezah* (the pure one).

Worried about her reputation sullying Salim's name, Sahibjaan takes to her heels again. Her destiny, she is convinced, is bound to the *kotha*, the only place which like a tomb will house the *zinda laash* (living corpse) that she feels she has become.

Salim feels hurt at her fleeing away like that and to spite her choice, he invites her to do a *mujra* at his wedding. In frenzy, she dances on broken glass --- scarring the feet he loved so much.

Finally, Shahabuddin learns that she is his daughter. He dies in the end being a target of his elder brother's bullet. But in his last moments, he takes a promise from Salim that he shall give a name of respect to his daughter by marrying her. Salim's *doli* defies all conventions and arrives at Sahibjaan's *kotha*, thus leading to a happy, emotion-charged

- Meena Kumari had worked under Kamal Amrohi's direction earlier in *Daera* (1953)

- Kamal Amrohi performed the *mahurat* of the film in February 1956. The film got stuck in 1964 when Meena and Kamal separated. A few years later, well-wishers like Sunil Dutt and Nargis advised them to restart the film.

- At the premiere of the film, Meena Kumari sat between Raaj Kumar and Kamal Amrohi and was very pleased with the film. When Khayyam complimented her by saying '*Shahkar ban gaya*', she was in tears.

- Meena Kumari was too ill to perform all the intricate *mujra* dances in the film. So actress Padma Khanna performed the climax song posing as Meena Kumari with a veil hiding her face. Amrohi shot the entire song '*Chalo dildaar chalo*' without showing her face. Her understated performance and moist eyes sparkling with unshed tears have a hypnotic effect

Jai Santoshi Maa **1975**

Director	🌀	Vijay Sharma
Producer	🌀	Satram Rohara (Bhagya Lakshmi ChitrMandir)
Starring	🌀	Bharat Bhushan
	🌀	Ashish Kumar, Anita Guha (as Santoshi Maa),
	🌀	Kanan Kaushal , Trilok Kapoor, Rajni Bala, Leela
	🌀	Mishra, B.M.Vyas, Rajan Haskar,
	🌀	Mahipal, Bela Bose, Asha Potdaar, Mahar Desai,
	🌀	Kundan, Neelam, Padmarani, Lata Arora, Johney
	🌀	Wishky, Tiwari, Dube,
Music	🌀	C. Arjun
Lyrics	🌀	Kavi Pradeep
Story	🌀	R. Priyadarshini
Cinematography	🌀	Sudhendu Roy
Release date(s)	🌀	1975
Running time	🌀	130 minutes
Language	🌀	Hindi (Colour)

Jai Santoshi Maa is the story of how a young woman overcomes various challenges in life through her firm devotion to *Santoshî Mâ* (also called *Santoshi Mata* or *Santoshi Maa*), a goddess of satisfaction. This movie released in the same year when

action and violence packed movies like *Sholay* and *Deewar* thrilled the hearts of Indian masses. And yet, despite such stiff competition, this simple movie based on mythology and religion not only became one of the biggest successes of the year, but actually popularised the worship of hitherto not a very well known Goddess.

With the birth of a new Goddess *Santoshi Maa* (played by Anita Guha), middle class women all over the country began fasting for the Goddess on twelve consecutive Fridays after seeing this film. The ladies in the cinema halls used to offer coins, petals and rice on 'Santoshi Maa' (Anita Guha) as soon as they heard the melodious *bhajans* like 'Main to aarti utaroon re' and 'Madad karo Santoshi Mata'. Some reports say that people at times used to take off their shoes outside the cinema halls before going in to see the film. Following the release of the film, *Santoshi Maa* has been worshipped as a Goddess on a large scale, particularly by urban women in northern India.

In the film, *Santoshi Maa* is depicted as a daughter of Ganesha, who is born to give her brothers a sister to tie *raakhi*. Ganesha himself is depicted as a householder with wives, sons, and a sister. As is the common belief in north India, his wives are Riddhi and Siddhi, and his sons are Shubha and Labha. The boys are unhappy because they, unlike Ganesha, have no sister. But Ganesha is not sure about having another child. The boys and the women plead with Ganesha, and the sage Nârada convinces him that having a daughter would be good. Ganesha assents and from Riddhi and Siddhi emerges a flame that engenders Santoshî Mâ.

The music and songs of the film were super hit and even the non-devotees found themselves humming them for a long time. These songs also helped the movie to break all time records of box office success and collections.

Memorable songs of 'Jai Santoshi Maa'

Song	*Singers*
→ *Main to aarti utaroon re Santoshi Maata ki*	Usha Mangeshkar and others
→ *Yahan wahan jahan kahan mat phoocho kahan kahan*	Mahender Kumar and others
→ *Mat ro mat ro aaj radhike*	Manna De
→ *Karti hoon tumhara vart main sweekar karo maa*	Usha Mangeshkar
→ *Madad karo Santodhi Mata*	Usha Mangeshkar
→ *Jai Jai Santoshi Mata*	Pradeep and others

Story

The film tells the story of Satyawati (Kanan Kaushal) who has an unwavering faith in *Santoshi Maa* and for whom she performs regular *vrats* (fasts). Her devotion and the powers of *Santoshi Maa* are severely tested by envious Goddesses (Brahmani, Laxmi and Parvati). Her husband (Ashish Kumar). goes away in search of work, and the envious Goddesses make him lose his  memory so that he forgets his wife. Satyawati is victimised and bullied by her in-laws. But she faces all these challenges patiently, maintaining her unflinching devotion in *Santoshi Maa*. Her faith is rewarded as, at every step, she is miraculously saved by her benevolent goddess. And in the end, she is finally restored to her husband, who returns home with riches to give his wife a comfortable life. Following her example, her entire family becomes devotees of *Santoshi Maa* in the end.

 ## Remarks

◉ He producer sold his wife's jewellery to complete the film which was repeatedly stalled due to lack of funds.

◉ The script for the film has no basis in Puranic legends or other known scriptures. In particular, the claims that Ganesha had a sister and a daughter appear to be unique to this film. In Maharashtra, there is a popular belief that Ganesha has a sister in each of the four directions and he goes to meet each of them annually on the occasion of Ganesha Chaturthi. But this is not the same myth as depicted in the film.

SHOLAY

Sholay **1975**

Director	●	Ramesh Sippy
Producer	●	G.P.Sippy
Story	●	Salim (Khan) Javed (Akhtar)
Starring	●	Dharmendra......... as Veeru
	●	Sanjeev Kumar.... as Thakur Baldev Singh
	●	Amitabh Bachchan..as Jaidev
	●	Amjad Khan....... as Gabbar Singh
	●	Hema Malini....... as Basanti
	●	Jaya Bhaduri...... as Radha
	●	Iftekhar............. as Radha's father
	●	Jagdeep............. as Surma Bhopali
	●	Asrani............... as the comic jailor
	●	Viju Khote.......... as Kalia
	●	Mac Mohan......... as Sambha
	●	A.K.Hangal........ as the blind Imam
	●	Sachin............... as Ahmed, the Imam's son
	●	Leela Mishra ....as mausi, Basanti's aunt
	●	Satyen Kappu ... as Ramlaal, Thakur's servant
	●	Helen................ as the sexy Gypsy dancer
	●	Jalal Agha........... as a Gypsy singer
Music	●	Rahul Dev Burman

Lyrics	◘	Anand Bakshi
Cinematography	◘	Dwarka Divecha
Release date(s)	◘	1975
Running time	◘	188 min./India:204min/USA:162 min
Language	◘	Hindi (Colour)

Sholay is one of the biggest blockbusters in the history of Hindi film industry. It was inspired by a film called *The Magnificent Seven. Sholay,* accepted as the greatest Hindi film of all times, is a movie that provides total entertainment, spiced up with every Bollywood masala, and unashamedly so. The movie has such universal appeal that even a lover of realistic cinema cannot help but be guilty of being entertained by its hundred percent pure, unadulterated drama. It appeals to everyone and, as it needs no cultural explanations,. is always a good choice to show to people who have never seen a Hindi film before.

Unsurprisingly, it is the highest grossing film of all times in India. In 1999, it was declared the "Film of the Millennium" by BBC India. It also won the title of the 'Best Film of 50 years' at the 50th Filmfare Awards in 2004.

When first released on August 15, 1975 in the Bombay region, the film was declared a commercial disaster. Audiences were light at first, and the critics were harsh. Trade journals and columnists called the expensive film a flop. But soon the cinema halls started to fill up. Word of mouth convinced movie-goers to give the film a chance and soon it became a box-office phenomenon. People weren't buying tickets in advance but they were coming to the theatre to see a film that their friends had liked. Before long, the film became a popular craze. All shows were sold out. At some theatres, the queue to ticket counters stretched more than a kilometre. Fans stood in line in pouring rains to buy tickets.

Sholay ran for more than five years. At Mumbai's Minerva theatre, it was shown in regular shows for three continuous years, and then in matinee shows for two more years. It racked up a record 60 golden jubilees across India, and doubled its original gross over reruns during the late 1970s, 1980s, 1990s and early 2000s. Even in the 240th week of its release, *Sholay* was showing to packed theatres.

Watching *Sholay* in theatres became something like a karaoke experience. There are some fans who saw the film thirty, forty, even a hundred times. Many fans in the audience had memorized all the dialogues and spoke them out loud, in chorus with the characters in the film. Some fans had even memorized the sound-effects.

At the time of release of the film, its songs did not attract the attention of masses but the dialogues did - a rarity for Bollywood. This prompted the producers to release audio-cassettes with only the popular dialogues like: '*Kitne aadmi the*', '*Tera kya hoga kaaliya*', '*Arre O sambha*', '*Chal Dhanno, aaj teri basanti ki izzat ka sawal hai*'. It was the first movie to release a cassette of its dialogue. The soundtrack was also widely appreciated for its instrumental scores that

No mention of the soundtrack is complete without a discussion of *'Mehbooba Mehbooba'*. This song displayed Burman's impressive vocal skills as a singer, and courage as a composer to introduce gypsy elements into Indian film music. This song has been highly anthologized, remixed, and recreated. Other songs of the movie also became popular, especially the song *'Yeh Dosti hum nahin todenge'* that almost became an anthem of friendship in India and is still serving the purpose.

Memorable songs of 'Sholay'

Song	Singers
→ O-jab tak hai jaan jaane jehan	Lata Mangeshkar
→ Koi haseena jab rooth jaati hai	Kishore Kumar and Hema Malini
→ Holi ke din, dil khil jaate hain	Kishore Kumar and Lata Mangeshkar
→ Yeh dosti hum nahin todenge	Kishore Kumar and Manna De
→ Mehbooba mehbooba	Rahul Dev Burman
A qawwali- Aa shru hota hai phir baharon ka mausam	Kishore Kumar, Manna De, Anand Bakshi, Bhupender and others *This song was recorded, but it was never picturised or released.*

Story

The movie starts with a train entering Chandanpur station. Ramlal, Thakur's servant, receives the Jailor, and takes him to Thakur's haveli. At their meeting, Thakur shows the Jailor a photograph of Veeru and Jaidev, two highly professional crooks. Thakur asks the jailor to find them out. He knows they are criminals, but his experience with them convinces him that they are also brave and good at heart. He wants them for a personal mission.

Thakur Baldev Singh (Sanjeev Kumar) is a retired police officer who, as a young officer, had captured the notorious outlaw Gabbar Singh (Amjad Khan) and had sent him to jail. Gabbar soon managed to escape from the prison and took his revenge by killling Thakur's entire family, with the exception of his daughter-in-law Radha (Jaya Bachchan) who was not at home at that moment. Later, Gabber also cut off Thakur's arms to leave him maimed for life. Unable to avenge his family's death himself, Thakur turns to the two small time crooks and jailbirds Jaidev (Amitabh Bachchan) and Veeru (Dharmendra), to capture Gabbar.

Once in the village, Jaidev and Veeru quickly adapt to their new life as protectors of the village. Both of them also fall in love. Veeru is attracted to Basanti (Hema Malini), a feisty woman who makes her living driving a *tanga* (horse drawn carriage). Jai is drawn to Radha (Jaya Bhaduri), the helpless widowed daughter-in-law of Thakur.

Veeru is a tough man with a soft heart while Jai is cool, quiet and composed but has a pungent sense of humour. They both love each other like brothers and are willing to even lay down their own life for the other's sake.

Veeru makes great show of his liking for Basanti and even climbs up drunk on a high water tank and threatens suicide to persuade Basanti's aunt (Leela Mishra) to get him married with Basanti. On the other hand, Jai's love for Radha is silent and patient. Radha and Jai have no conversation throughout the film, but they communicate through silence.

Conflicts between Jai, Veeru and Gabbar Singh's men continue. Veeru is captured and to save his life, Basanti (Hema) is forced to dance before Gabbar Singh on fragments of broken glass. Bloody clashes between Jai, Veeru, and the bandits follow. Ultimately, the bandits are slain and peace and security prevails in the end. But this peace has come at a heavy price. Jai loses his life in the struggle and with him dies the love that had started budding in the forlorn heart of Radha as well.

The film has two known endings. The original ending (shown in the Eros-released DVD) has Thakur Baldev Singh killing Gabbar Singh, trampling him with spike-soled shoes. The Censor Board of India, however, found the ending unacceptable as they thought that police officers or even ex-police officers should not be shown to commit murder. A new ending was filmed, in which the police arrest Gabbar Singh in the nick of time. Several other minor changes were made as well. Barring the ending, the two versions of the film are mostly the same.

Remarks

- Sanjeev Kumar wanted to play Gabbar Singh, but the producers insisted that he play the police officer. Dharmendra was interested in playing Gabbar Singh as well, but changed his mind when Ramesh Sippy told him Basanti was to be played by Hema Malini.
- The director's original choice for Jaidev too was different. Shatrughan Sinha was almost signed, when Dharmendra convinced the producers that Amitabh would be the right choice.
- The producers wanted Danny Denzongpa to play the bandit chief, but he was committed to Feroz Khan's *Dharmatma.* Amjad Khan was a second choice.
- The scene in which Thakur's family is killed was cut by the Censor Board; the murder of a small child was deemed too horrific to show.

● The film showcased two real life romances. Amitabh married Jaya Bhaduri, who played the widowed daughter-in-law, in 1973, during the filming. Dharmendra married Hema Malini in 1980, five years after the release of the film.

● Amjad Khan prepared to play a bandit chief by reading a book titled 'Abhishapth Chambal', which told of the exploits of Chambal dacoits. The book was written by Taroon Bhaduri, who happened to be the father of Jaya Bhaduri. MacMohan is most remembered for his role as the dacoit Sambha, though the character had only one dialogue in the whole film.

● It was the first Hindi (and possibly Indian) movie to have a stereophonic soundtrack and to succeed in 70mm.

● Consolidating the multi-star trend, it gave more immortal characters than any single film, ran for 150 weeks in regular shows and proved the biggest hit ever in Indian celluloid history.

● Amjad Khan as Gabbar Singh became the first-ever villain to be loved even by the children.

● The film was a lavish production for its time. It took two and a half years to make.

● Much of the film was set in the rocky terrain of Ramanagaram, a village near Banglore. The filmmakers had to build a road from the Bangalore highway to Ramanagaram for convenient access to the sets. In fact, one part of Ramanagaram town was renamed 'Sippynagar' after the director of the movie. Even to this day, a visit to the 'Sholay rocks' (where the movie was shot) is offered to tourists travelling through Ramanagaram (on the road between Bangalore and Mysore).

● Sholay's extensive use of slow-motion in shoot-outs was influenced by the westerns of Sam Peckinpah, films such as *The Wild Bunch* (1969) and *Pat Garrett* and *Billy the Kid* (1973).

● The first film to show a village hiring mercenaries to protect itself from bandits was the Japanese director Akira Kurosawa's *Seven Samurai*. Hollywood remade it as *The Magnificent Seven* in 1960, fifteen years before *Sholay*. Indian films *Mera Gaon Mera Desh* (1971) and *Khote Sikkay* (1973) might have served as some inspiration as well.

● Gabbar Singh was modelled on a real-life dacoit of the same name who menaced the villages around Gwalior in the 1950s. He terrorized the local police. Any policeman captured by the real Gabbar Singh had his ears and nose cut off, and was then released as lesson to other policemen.

● The train robbery sequence took about twenty days to shoot. It was shot at the Bomba-Pune line, near Panvel.

Legacy

- *Sholay* has inspired many imitations in cinema and television but non of them has touched the heights and success of the film. Even the film *Ram Gopal Varma Ki Aag* based on the storyline of *Sholay*, released with much publicity in August 2007 proved to be an utter disaster.

- The super success of *Sholay* spurred the careers of its lead stars like Amitabh Bachchan and Dharmendra, but put a heavy load on the careers of the junior and supporting actors. They never truly escaped the shadow of this film and their characters in it.

- Amjad Khan, who played the bandit Gabbar Singh played many more villainous roles afterwards, including Gabbar Singh again in 1991 in the film *Ramgarh Ke Sholay*.

- Comedian Jagdeep, who played Soorma Bhopali in the film, also attempted to capitalize on his *Sholay* success. He directed and played the lead role in the 1988 film *Soorma Bhopali*, in which Dharmendra and Amitabh Bachchan also played cameos. The film however flopped.

Hum Aapke Hain Koun..! 1994

Director	● Sooraj R. Barjatya
Producer	● Ajit Kumar Barjatya
	● Kamal Kumar Barhatya (Rajshree Productions)
	● Rajkumar Barhatya
Story	● Sooraj R. Barjatya
Starring	● Salman Khan as Prem, Madhuri Dixit as Nisha
	● Mohnish Behl as Rajesh, Renuka Shahane as Pooja
	● Anupam Kher as Prof. Siddharth Choudhury
	● Reema Lagoo as Mrs. Choudhury (as Rima)
	● Alok Nath as Kailashnath (Prem's father-like uncle)
	● Bindu as Aunt, Ajit Vachani as Aunt's Husband,
	● Satish Shah as Doctor
	● Himani Shivpuri as Razia (The Doctor's wife)
	● Sahila Chaddha as Rita
	● Dilip Joshi as Bhola Prasad
	● Laxmikant Berde as Lalloo Prasad
	● Priya Arun as Chanda
	● Tuffy as Tuffy (The Dog)
Music	● Raam Laxman
Lyrics	● Dev Kohli, Ravinder Rawal
Cinematography	● Rajan Kinagi

diting	❖	Mukhtar Ahmed
istributed by	❖	Rajshri Productions
	❖	Eros Entertainment (DVD)
	❖	Digital Entertainment (VCD)
elease year	❖	1994
unning time	❖	206 min.
anguage	❖	Hindi (Colour)

Hum Aapke Hain Kaun...! is one of the biggest grossers ever produced in the ndian Film Industry. Directed by Sooraj Barjatya, it is one of the most successful Bollywood lms ever. It's a film about love, respect, family values and relationships, filled with three nd half hours of healthy entertainment and laborate song and dance sequences.

This film came when lots of careers were at take. Salman Khan had been written off by many. 1adhuri Dixit was being married off to Dr Sriram Nene. 1 fact, the couple had already tied the knot at a private eremony in Los Angeles on October 17. But the film reated history and changed the course of individual ates at one go.

Hum Aapke Hain Kaun...! is a story of two ndian families and the relationships between them, elebrating Indian culture and its values. It is noted for s lavish depiction of North Indian wedding eremonies.

It's a remake of the 1982 Hindi film *Nadiya Ke aar* by Rajshri Productions. In keeping with the ajshri tradition of no sex and violence, the Barjatiyas id not once move away from the formula. The film ffers clean entertainment for the whole family. It was lso dubbed into Telugu as *Premalayam* and become a ilver jubliee (25 weeks) film in Tollywood.

Its popular soundtrack, including an unusually large number of songs, was scored by aam Laxman. All the songs of this movie became a huge hit, but in particular the song '*Didi tera evar deewana*' became an instant rage and a must in every wedding celebration. So much so hat even the *saree* that Madhuri Dixit wore for this particular song became a fashion trend.

Story

Hum Aapke hain Kaun..! is the story of two lovers, Prem (Salman han) and Nisha (Madhuri Dixit). They meet at the engagement of Prem's

brother Rajesh (Mohnish Behl) with Nisha's sister Pooja (Renuka Shahane). Pooja and Nisha are daughters of Professor

Choudhary (Anupam Kher) and Kamla Devi (Reema Lagoo). Prem and Rajesh's parents are dead but they have been brought up by their uncle Kailashnath (Alok Nath).

Rajesh (Mohnish Behl) and Pooja (Renuka Shahane) get married, and the functions include a long wedding ceremony where the rituals spread out over two songs.

Pooja finds a lot of affection at her husband's home and everybody is happy. Prem and Nisha fall in love with each other when Nisha comes to stay for the birth of Pooja's baby. Prem tells his sister-in-law, Nisha's older sister Pooja, that he loves Nisha. Pooja binds the two with her blessings and a necklace. Before Pooja can tell anyone the good news, she falls down the stairs and dies. Everyone feels numb with grief after Pooja dies, because she was an affectionate and caring person who loved and was loved by every member of the family. Rajesh finds life hard without Pooja, and is worried about his son who has lost his mother at such tender age. The elders of the family decide to get Rajesh married to Nisha so that he won't feel so lonely, and his son will get a mother. Nisha unknowingly accepts because she mistakenly thinks that it is Prem her

parents are discussing about as her future husband. When she finds out that she is marrying Rajesh, she is heart broken. But she soon realizes why her parents took the decision and considering it her duty to take care of her sister's child and husband, she tells Prem to forget her.

The wedding day arrives and it is now certain that Nisha will marry Rajesh, sacrificing her love for Prem. Prem too thinks that he owes this sacrifice to his elder brother. The only person who knows how much Prem and Nisha love each other is Prem's servant. He prays to God to stop the edding and get Prem and Nisha married. God works his miracle through Tuffy, the dog. The dog ulls out the necklace that Pooja had gifted to Nisha when she had learnt of Prem and Nisha's eelings for each other. Nisha now decides to return this necklace back to Prem with a note that nentions the end of their love. The dog takes the necklace and the note and instead of giving it to Prem, he gives it to Rajesh. Rajesh finds out that Nisha and Prem love each other, and teps aside so that his younger brother can marry Nisha. In the end, all confusions are cleared nd the loving hearts of Prem and Nisha unite to live happily ever after.

Awards

National Awards

- Best Popular Film Providing wholesome entertainment
- Swarna Kamal and Rs.40,000/-each to Producer and Director
- Best Choreography: Rajat Kamal and Rs.10,000/- to Jay Borade

Filmfare Awards

- Best Film
- Best Director
- Best Actress (Madhuri Dixit)

Screen Awards

- Best Film
- Best Director
- Best Actor (Female)
- Best Film
- Best Screenplay
- Best Editing
- Best Playback Singer (Female)

DILWALE
DULHANIYA
LE
JAYENGE

Dilwale Dulhaniya Le Jayenge 1995

Director	❂	Aditya Chopra
Producer	❂	Yash Chopra (Yash Raj Films)
Story	❂	Aditya Chopra
	❂	Javed Siddiqui
Starring	❂	Shahrukh Khan…as Raj Malhotra
	❂	Kajol …………… as Simran
	❂	Amrish Puri……. as Chaudhry Baldev Singh
	❂	Farida Jalal ……..as Lajwanti
	❂	Anupam Kher….. as Dharamvir Malhotra
	❂	Satish Shah …….as Ajit Singh
	❂	Achala Sachdev.. as Simran's grandmother
	❂	Himani Shivpuri.. as Kammo
	❂	Pooja Ruparel….. as Rajeshwari / Chutki
	❂	Hemlata Deepak.. as Sheena
	❂	Arjun Sablok…… as Rocky
	❂	Karan Johar……. as Robby
	❂	Parmeet Sethi….. as Kuljeet
	❂	Mandira Bedi…. as Preeti
Music	❂	Jatin Lalit
Lyrics	❂	Anand Bakshi

Cinematography	⊙	Manmohan Singh
Editing	⊙	Keshav Naidu
Distributed by	⊙	Yash Raj Films
Release date(s)	⊙	October 20,1995
Running time	⊙	189 min.
Language	⊙	Hindi (Colour)

Dilwale Dulhania Le Jayenge or *DDLJ* as it is also known, was Aditya Chopra's directorial debut. It became an instant super hit. It premiered on October 19, 1995 and was released nationwide on October 20, 1995. As of April 2007, the film had made a record by completing 600 weeks of continuous play in Maratha Mandir, in Mumbai. The film was included in the Cinema India showcase, *The Changing Face of Indian Cinema,* which toured the United States in July and August 2004.

Filmed in Switzerland, it was one of the first Bollywood films based on Indians living outside India and it was also the first film to establish Shahrukh Khan as a romantic hero. The character of Raj Malhotra (Shahrukh Khan) was categorically explained to Shahrukh by the director Aditya. He wanted Raj to have the feelings of a teenager and the maturity of an adult. He was to be a spoiled brat who failed in his examinations, never reached anywhere on time, guzzled beers and didn't hesitate in tricking people for his own convenience. And yet, he's also the man who loves his father, respects women and familial ties, and would rather labour at winning the hearts of his beloved's parents instead of eloping off with their daughter against their wishes.

The movie starred Kajol as Simran and Amrish Puri as Simran's strict father. Actress Mandira Bedi and Parmeet Sethi were introduced in this film. The Non-Resident Indian's experience came to the fore as Raj followed Simran from England to a village in Punjab to discover his roots and romance. The film is peppered with fisticuffs, comic interludes, and a stern father insisting on an arranged marriage that add to the drama of the movie and make it a wholesome entertainer.

The movie also boasts of super hit musical tracks that compelled the nation to sing along as Raj and Simran romanced with each other in the movie.

Memorable songs of 'Dilwale Dulhaniya le jayenge'

Song

➡ *Mehndi laga ke rakhna, doli saza ke rakhna.*
➡ *Mere khawabo mein jo aaye, aa ke mujhe ched jaye*
➡ *Na jaane mere dil ko kya ho gaya*
➡ *Tujhe dekha to ye jana sanam*
➡ *Ruk ja o dil diwane*
➡ *Zara sa jhoom loon main*
➡ *Ghar aa ja pardesi*

 **Story**

Chaudhry Baldev Singh (Amrish Puri) is a London based immigrant from India. He, along with his wife Lajwanti (Farida Jalal) and two daughters Simran (Kajol) and Chutki (Pooja Ruparel), has been living in London for the past several years. A true Indian at heart, Chaudhry Baldev Singh is a man of great morals and has tried to imbibe the same in his daughters. He has brought them up with the belief that they are strangers in this foreign land and must remain true to their Indian values and traditions. He intends to return one day back to Punjab- back to his roots, his land, his culture that he so strongly believes in.

Simran, like any other girl her age, dreams of this perfect man and waits for him to walk into her life. However, she soon realises the futility of all her dreams. She knows that when she was just a child, her father had fixed her marriage with his best friend's son. She realizes that it's time to give up all her dreams when a letter from India arrives reminding them of that promise and urging them to return to India so that the marriage could be solemnised.

On the other hand Raj Malhotra (Shahrukh Khan), another London based immigrant, is a rich and spoilt brat brought up in the lap of luxury. He is a true playboy at heart. But he shares a beautiful relationship with his father Dharamvir Malhotra (Anupam Kher). They are more like friends.

Simran's friends want her to accompany them on a graduation trip. She pleads with her father and finally manages to get his permission. It is on this very trip that she meets Raj. After some initial misadventures, they come close and fall in love. They, however, realise their true feelings for each other only when they part at the end of the trip.

Just when they are about to part ways, Simran asks Raj for his address so that she could send her wedding invitation to him. He gives the address but tells her '*Main nahin aaoonga*'. She realizes that it means that she would never see him again. This thought weighs heavily on her heart and makes her realize how much she loves him.

She goes home and tells her family about Raj. Her father is enraged. He is adamant that she marry his best friend's son Kuljeet (Parmeet Sethi), to whom she has been promised since she was born. He makes an impulsive decision to leave for Punjab overnight. Simran's mother wants to help her, but cannot sway the will of her domineering father.

Meanwhile Raj, who too cannot stop thinking about Simran, is motivated by his father who tells him that if he truly loves Simran, he has to go and get her. Unfortunately, by the time Raj reaches her home, she has already left for India. Raj, however, does not give up so easily. He follows Simran to Punjab and meeting her privately, assures her that he will save her from the forced marriage. She pleads to him to take her away immediately but he refuses to elope with Simran because he wants everyone to be happy with the marriage. He wants to marry her with the consent of her father.

He manages to come close to Kuljeet, the soon-to-be groom, who is a man full of himself and thinks he is a *Punjab ka sher* (tiger). He cunningly plays upon Kuljeet's greed and befriends him, thereby coming close to his family. With his charming style, he wins his way into the hearts of Chaudhry Baldev Singh's family as well. Raj helps with the wedding preparations and soon gains everyone's friendship and love. At the same time Kuljeet's unmarried sister (Mandira Bedi) gets attracted towards Raj and it gets more complicated when Raj's father suddenly appears on the scene and agrees to the marriage, thinking her to be the Simran whom Raj loves. By now, even Simran's father is won over by Raj's charm.

However, everything comes crashing down when Simran's father sees a photograph of Raj and Simran and Raj's true identity is revealed. Then, as Raj is preparing to leave, Kuljeet comes up on the railway station and beats him up for playing games with him. He even hits Raj's father which incites Raj to fight back. However, when Simran's father interrupts the fight, he

relents and without raising any complaint or accusation prepares to leave.

Fortunately, just when the train is speeding away, with Raj on it, Simran's father realizes the depth and sincerity of Raj's love and allows Simran to leave with Raj as well. Raj sees her coming and leans out of the train to grasp her extended hand as she runs towards him. Their hands meet, and he pulls her up on the train with him. In the end, *Dilwale*- the boy with a heart full of love- finally manages to take away *Dulhania* -his bride.

Remarks

- .*Dilwale Dulhania Le Jayenge,* which was a critical and commercial success, has entered its twelfth year at Maratha Mandir, a cinema Hall in Mumbai, and has grossed nearly twelve billion rupees in all.
- In October 2006, the Consulate General of Switzerland and Switzerland Tourism in Mumbai organised a formal dinner to congratulate the stars and producers of the movie for its record-breaking long run in Mumbai.
- Raj's (Shahrukh Khan) two friends Robby and Rocky are played by Karan Johar and Arjun Sablok, both of whom later became film directors.

Awards

Filmfare Awards

- Best Movie   (Yash Chopra)
- Best Director   (Aditya Chopra)
- Best Actor   (Shahrukh Khan)
- Best Actress   (Kajol)
- Best Supporting Actress   (Farida Jalal)
- Best Comedian   (Anupam Kher)
- Best Lyricist   (Anand Bakshi for the song '*Tujhe dekha*')
- Best Male Playback   (Udit Narayan for the song '*Mehndi lagake rakhna*')

National Awards

- Swarna Kamal and Rs.40,000/-each to the Producer and Director for the Best Popular Film providing wholesome entertainment.

Lagaan 2001

Director	Ashutosh Gowariker
Producer	Aamir Khan (Aamir Khan Productions)
Original Story	Ashutosh Gowariker
Screenplay	Kumar Dave, Sanjay Dayma
	and Ashutosh Gowariker
Dialogue	K.P. Saxena
Starring	AamirKhan......... as Bhuvan
	Gracy Singh.........as Gauri
	Rachel Shelley.....as Elizabeth Russell
	Paul Blackthorne..as Captain Andrew Russell
	Suhasini Mulay as Yashodamai
	Kulbhushan Kharbanda....as Raja Puran Singh
	Raghuvir Yadav....as Bhura
	Rajesh Vivek.........as Guran
	Raj Zutshi............as Ismail
	Pradeep Rawat......as Deva
	Daya Shankar Pandey..as Goli
	Yashpal Sharma....as Lakha
	Amin Hajee..........as Bagha
	Aditya Lakhia.......as Kachra
	A.K. Hangal.........as Shambhu Kaka

Music	A. R. Rahman
Lyrics	Javed Akhtar
Art	Nitin Desai
Cinematography	Anil Mehta
Editing	Ballu Saluja
Release date(s)	June 1, 2001
Running time	224 min
Language	Hindi, English, Bhojpuri (Colour)

Lagaan (English translation *land tax*) is an award-winning film, released on June 1, 2001. The full title of the movie is *Lagaan: Once upon a time in India.* It is a story of the common man's fight against oppression. A group of unlikely heroes rises up against injustice and with courage and indomitable will defeat the tyrant powers. A battle is fought and won without spilling a single drop of blood.

Lagaan became the third Hindi language film to be nominated for the Academy Award in the Best Foreign Language Film category (after *Mother India* in 1957 and *Salaam Bombay* in 1989). The director, Ashutosh Gowariker, and the lead actor and producer, Aamir Khan, flew to Los Angeles to lobby for the film. They, and the film, attracted a great deal of publicity. As a result, *Lagaan* was booked into many theatres worldwide, even in those theatres that do not ordinarily show Indian films. This was for many Westerners the first opportunity to see a genuine Bollywood film in the local cinema.

Lagaan was appreciated by one and all for its superb narrative, arresting storyline and brilliant performances by every member of the cast. The entire film was shot at Bhuj in Gujarat. Its bleak landscape has been beautifully captured on camera and the life of the place, as it must have been during British Raj, has been authentically recreated in the film. Adding to the popularity of *Lagaan* was its music. While the background music enhanced the drama of the movie, all the songs touched the heights of popularity and became chart busters. Penned by Javed Akhtar and composed by A. R. Rahman, the songs rang with rustic innocence as they sometimes called for succour from the merciless clouds *'Ghanan ghanan ghir ghir aaye badra'* or begged for help from the merciful God *'O Palanhare, nirgun aur nyare'*. While some songs melted the heart with joy of budding love- *'O ree chhori, maan bhi le baat mori'*, others moved with their call for action against the oppressive forces- *'Bar Bar haan, bolo yaar haan'*. But they all had two things in common, melody and brilliant choreography, that made them such a treat to listen and watch.

Memorable songs of '**Lagaan**'

Ghanan ghanan ghir ghir aaye badra
Sun mitva har sant kahe har sadhu kahe
Radha kaise na jale
O ree chhori, maan bhi le baat mori
O Palanhare, nirgun aur nyare
Bar Bar haan, bolo yaar haan

Story

Lagaan is set in the year 1895 in Champaner village in India. People of this village depended on agriculture as the main source of their livelihood. As in the other princely states of British India, the villagers had to pay an agricultural tax (*Lagaan*) to the British. The unsympathetic and arrogant commanding officer of the British cantonment in Champaner, Captain Andrew Russell (Paul Blackthorne), oppresses the people of the region with exorbitant taxes. The local ruler, Rajah Pooran Singh, tries to get the taxes lowered in order to ease the suffering of the drought-stricken villagers. But Captain Russell humiliates the *Rajah* by asking him to eat meat if he wishes the taxes to be lowered. The *Rajah*, being a religious man and a strict vegetarian, refuses. Captain Russell takes this refusal as his personal insult and in retaliation doubles the taxes.

The peasants, who are already suffering from a prolonged drought, are devastated by this news. For yet another year, the monsoon season has come and gone without shedding a drop of rain. The crops have all dried up and the villagers know that if it doesn't rain, their children will starve. They keep on watching the sky, hoping to catch the sight of rain clouds, but they appear and fly away without raining. Because of the drought, the poor villagers find themselves unable to pay even the regular taxes, leave alone the double *lagaan.* They decide to go to the Rajah and beg him to help them, though the Rajah himself is helpless and cannot persuade the British to mercy.

When the villagers go to meet the *Rajah*, they have to wait since the British officers are playing cricket. Captain Russell notices them and sees the young Bhuvan (Aamir Khan), who has angered him on an earlier occasion. This time Bhuvan calls their game a worthless sport, which further infuriates the Captain. In his

Cunning style, he puts forth a challenge before Bhuvan, and offers him a deal where he would cancel the taxes of the whole province for three years if a village team can beat the British officers at cricket. But the rider is that if the villagers lose, they will have to pay three times the tax. The other villagers are not allowed to speak, and they are horrified when Bhuvan accepts this challenge on their behalf.

The villagers of Champaner, and of all the neighbouring villages, are furious at Bhuvan. No one has ever played cricket. Not one of them even knows anything about this game. And it seems like a suicidal foolishness to everybody to even imagine a team of complete novices playing against the British. But Bhuvan is confident, and he explains that since they cannot pay the taxes, they should grab this chance for a tax remission. It was a God sent opportunity for them, and it was not impossible for them to learn the game, and even defeat the British officers. This way, he encourages them one by one to join him in his fight against British injustice.

The British Government, on learning of Captain Russell's offer, admonishes him for his arrogant and irresponsible behaviour. His superiors tell him that if he loses the match, he will have to reimburse all the taxes from his own pocket and moreover, would be punished with a transfer to East Africa.

A cricket team of novice villagers, led by the courageous Bhuvan and helped by Russell's good-hearted sister Elizabeth (Rachel Shelley), begins to learn cricket. Elizabeth's sense of fair play persuades her to oppose her brother by coaching the village team. As time progresses, more and more villagers are convinced to join Bhuvan's team. Bhuvan accepts them on merit alone, making them unite against the enemy by disregarding all considerations of religion and caste. This is controversial, but eventually accepted by the villagers. The team works hard and it seems that they might have a chance to win.

As they spend time together, Elizabeth falls in love with Bhuvan, who is himself attached to a charming local girl, Gauri (Gracy Singh). Gauri realizes that Elizabeth is in love with Bhuvan and feels very jealous. Her feelings of love and jealousy are beautifully brought out in the song 'Radha kaise na jale'. Bhuvan, however, feels nothing but respect for Elizabeth. Elizabeth never expresses her feelings but Gauri sees how matters stand and is anxious until Bhuvan declares his love to her.

This infuriates the woodcutter Lakha, who had hoped to make Gauri his own bride. Lakha becomes jealous with Bhuvan and to spite him, he goes and conspires with Captain Russell. The captain orders him to join Bhuvan's team as his informer. So Lakha joins the team, but secretly meets with Captain Russell, informing him of everything that is happening. The captain tries to prevent his sister Elizabeth from helping the villagers, but she defies him. Soon comes the time for the all important three-day Cricket match.

An immense crowd of villagers gathers to watch the game. After many ups and downs and thrilling moments in the game, the village eleven ultimately wins the match.

At the end of the film, the narrator states that Elizabeth, after coming to know that Bhuvan loved Gauri and not her, returned to England, where she never married and remained *"Bhuvan's Radha for all of her life"*. This suggests that, despite his marriage to Gauri, Elizabeth feels she and Bhuvan are united by a sacred bond. Her brother, Captain Russell is made to reimburse the taxes from his personal fortune and is posted to Africa as a punishment.

Awards

National Awards

- Best Popular Film Providing Wholesome Entertainment
- Best Music Direction- A. R. Rahman
- Best Male Playback Singer- Udit Narayan for the song *"Mitwa Re"*
- Best Audiography- H. Sridhar, Nakul Kamte
- Best Lyrics- Javed Akhtar
- Best Costume Design- Bhanu Anthaiya
- Best Art Direction- Nitin Chandrakant Desai

Filmfare Awards

- Best Actor - Aamir Khan
- Best Director - Ashutosh Gowarikar
- Best Film
- Best Music Director - A. R. Rahman
- Best Lyricist - Javed Akhtar
- Best Playback Singer (Male) - Udit Narayan for the song *"Mitwa Re"*
- Best Playback Singer (Female) - Alka Yagnik for the song *"O Re Chhori"*
- Best Story - Ashutosh Gowariker

Screen Awards

- Best Screenplay- Ashutosh Gowarikar, Kumar Dave, Sanjay Dayma
- Best Editing- Ballu Saluja
- Best Cinematography- Anil Mehta
- Best Art Direction- Nitin Chandrakant Desai
- Most Promising Newcomer (Female) - Gracy Singh
- Best Director- Ashutosh Gowariker
- Best Film
- Best Female Playback - Asha Bhosle for the song *"Radha kaise na jale"*.

IIFA Awards

- Best Actor - Aamir Khan
- Best Director - Ashutosh Gowariker
- Best Movie - Ashutosh Gowariker
- Best Playback Singer (Female) - Asha Bhosle for the song "*Radha kaise na jale*".
- Best Music Director - A. R. Rahman

ZEE Cine Awards

- Best Actor (Male) - Aamir Khan
- Best Female Debut - Gracy Singh
- Best Director - Ashutosh Gowariker
- Best Film - Ashutosh Gowariker
- Best Lyricist - Javed Akhtar for the song "*Radha kaise na jale*".
- Best Music Director - A.R. Rahman
- Best Playback Singer (Female) - Asha Bhosle for the song "*Radha kaise na jale*".
- Best Story - Ashutosh Gowarikar

Other Awards

- 2001 Bergen International Film Festival, Jury Award - Ashutosh Gowarikar
- 2002 Leeds International Film Festival, Audience Award - Ashutosh Gowariker
- 2002 Prix du Public (Audience Award)
- 54th Locarno International Film Festival in Switzerland
- 2002 Portland International Film Festival, Audience Award - Ashutosh Gowarikar

BAGHBAN

Baghban 2003

Director		Ravi Chopra
Story and Producer		B.R.Chopra (B.R.Films)
Starring		Amitabh Bachchan.. as Raj Malhotra
		Hema Malini.......as Pooja Malhotra
		Salman Khan......as Alok Raj
		(Special Appearance)
		Mahima Chaudhry as Arpita Raj
		(Special Appearance)
		Aman Verma...... as Ajay Malhotra
		Rimi Sen............ as Payal Malhotra
		Samir Soni......... as Sanjay Malhotra
		Saahil Chadda ... as Rohit Malhotra
		Nasir Khan ....as Karan Malhotra
		Divya Dutta ....as Reena Malhotra
		Suman Ranganathan ...as Kiran Malhotra
		Paresh Rawal......as Hemant Patel
		Lilette Dubey, Asrani, Awtaar Gill,
		Mohan Joshi
Director of Photography		Barun Mukherjee
Screenplay		Achla Nagar
Music		Uttam Singh, Adeish Srivastava
Lyrics		Sameer

Distributed by	◯	B.R.Films
Release date(s)	◯	October 3, 2003
Language	◯	Hindi (Colour)

Baghban   Is a 2003 Hindi film whose chief protagonists are not young lovebirds but two aging people.

Directed by Ravi Chopra, the movie raises the question that if parents can help their child in the first steps of his or her life, then why can't that very child help the parents in the last few steps of their lives.

It's a story about sacrifices that parents make, about their expectations from their children, and finally about how, too often, these expectations come to nothing. The movie revolves around a man who has brought up four sons but finds no place for himself and his wife in any of their posh residences. A man who has dedicated his life to the upbringing of his children, finds himself being treated like a burden in the life of these very children. A man who tried to inculcate in his offspring the lessons of love and dedication, finds himself being separated from his wife the love of his life, because his sons cannot *afford* to take care of both of them together in their old age. But despite all this, *Baghban* is not a story of helpless old age. It's story of aging with dignity and pride and fighting against the humiliation meted out by one's own children.

It's a remarkable film, for the novelty of its theme, the delicately poised storyline, the deliciousness of the mature love of the aging couple, the power-packed performances by the cast and finally, the music. Almost all the songs of this movie became chart-busters. Amitabh Bachchan himself gave voice to three of the songs. While all of these three songs became popular, the song 'main yahan tu wahan' was especially appreciated for its soulful melody and the emotions that Amitabh Bachchan was able to bring out while singing this song.

Memorable songs of 'Baghban'

Song	Singers
Meri makhna meri soniye	Sudesh Bhosle and Alka Yagnik
Pehele kabhi na mera haal	Udit Narayan and Alka Yagnik
Holi khele raghuvira	Amitabh Bachchan, Sukwinder Singh and Alka Yagnik
Main yahan tu wahan	Amitabh Bachchan and Alka Yagnik
O dharti tarse ambar barse	Amitabh Bachchan and Richa Sharma
Chali chali phir chali	Amitabh Bachchan, Adesh Srivastava,Hema Sardesai and Alka Yagnik.

Story

The title of the movie is *Baghban* which means a gardener. A gardener plants a tree and nurses it in the hope that he would be able to bask in its shade when he grows old The movie too revolves around a father who, just like a gardener, dedicates all his life and life's savings for the well being of his sons, believing that in the time of his need, his sons would be there to help and support him.

The movie tells the story of Raj Malhotra (Amitabh Bachchan) and his wife Pooja (Hema Malini) and their four sons Ajay (Aman Verma), Sanjay (Samir Soni), Rohit (Saahil Chadda), and Karan (Nasir Khan).

Raj and Pooja have provided their children with every facility and abundance of love. These children are now nicely settled in their respective professions. Their life is filled with love and prosperity and all this has been possible because Raj has invested all his income, including his provident fund and gratuity, in his children who, according to him, are his assets that would secure his future.

Raj Malhotra also has an adopted son Alok (Salman Khan). Alok is an orphan whom Raj had helped with money and education.

Now a successful man, he worships Raj because of all the help and support that this generous man had given him. Alok realises that without the benign support of Raj, he would most probably have remained an uneducated and poor orphan living off the streets. Alok has a very loving and good natured fiancée, Arpita (Mahima Chaudhary).

Raj has been a much respected employee in his office. And now that he's retired, he and Pooja decide to live with their kids and spend the rest of their life sharing their love and happiness. They let their children know of their decision. What follows this declaration gives them a rude shock and leaves them stunned.

None of the four sons is ready to take their parents' responsibility. They don't want them interfering in their lives and freedom. They know that Raj and Pooja love each other so much that they would never agree to live apart from each other. So, to be freed of the responsibility of their parents, the children propose just such a separation. One son invites the mother while the other son is ready to take care of the father for six months. After the end of six months, Raj and Pooja would have to move to the homes of the remaining two sons, still to live away from each other. Their children believe that Raj and Pooja would never agree to such an arrangement, and hence they'd be freed of the bother of keeping them altogether.

But Raj and Pooja, after much deliberation, agree to give this plan a try. They move out of their rented home and start living separatly with their sons. They soon realize how unwanted they are in the homes of their own kids. The movie poignantly shows how they endure being separated from each other and face horrible treatment from their own children. Their condition becomes so pathetic that Raj and Pooja have to depend on the kindness of strangers.

Saddened by the treatment he has received from his children and their families, Raj Malhotra starts writing a book about his own life. He befriends a coffee shop owner who sends his book to a publisher. Meanwhile, Raj and Pooja have had enough of the humiliation at hands of their own offsprings. They leave their sons' homes

nd find shelter in the home of their dopted child Alok. They receive much ve and respect from him and Arpita, ho's now his wife.

Soon, his book, titled *Baghban,* released. This book resonates with the uestion that if a man helps his children 1 the early days of their lives, why can't hese very children take care of him in he last days of his life.

The book becomes an instant uccess and Raj gains much fame and nce again becomes financially ndependent. At the book release unction, all his sons show up to bask in he glow of their father's fame. But he refuses to acknowledge them and instead recognizes Alok s his only son. The movie ends with Raj Malhotra coming out as a winner and once again egaining the hold of his life and beginning a new journey forward, with dignity and with pride.

 *Remarks*

- B.R.Chopra initially wanted to make this movie thirty years ago. He wanted Dilip Kumar and Raakhee to play the lead roles.
- Mohnish Behl was offered Aman Verma's role but he did not accept it because he did not want to be portrayed as the father of a fifteen-year-old girl.
- Amitabh Bachchan sang three songs himself. He and Hema Malini were paired opposite each other after twenty years since they last worked together in *Nastik* in 1983.
The movie is a remake of a National award winning Kannada movie *Post Master*.
- This movie is also the remake of the Marathi movie *Tu Thitha Me*, meaning *'Where You Are There I Am'*.

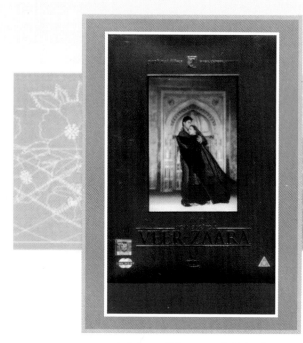

Veer Zara **2004**

Director	Yash Chopra
Producer	Yash Chopra, Aditya Chopra (Yash Raj Films)
Story, Screenplay and Dialogue	Aditya Chopra
Starring	Shahrukh Khan as Squadron Leader Veer Pratap Singh
	Preity Zinta as…. Zaara Haayat Khan
	Rani Mukerji as…….Saamiya
	SiddiquAmitabh Bachchan as …..Chaudhary
	Sumer Singh (Bauji)
	Hema Malini as…..Saraswati Kaur (Maati)
	Kirron Kher as…… Mariam Haayat Khan
	Divya Dutta as….Shabbo
	Boman Irani as….Jahangir Haayat Khan
	Manoj Bajpai as…. Razaa Shirazi
	Anupam Kher as.. Zakir Ahmed
Music	Late Madan Mohan (Sanjeev Kohli)
Lyrics	Javed Akhtar
Cinematography	Anil Mehta ISC
Distributed by	Yash Raj Films
Editor	Retesh Soni
Release date(s)	November 12, 2004
Running time	192 min.
Language	Hindi/Urdu/Punjabi (colour)

Veer-Zaara is a saga of love that spans across two countries and remains strong even after the separation of two decades. It's a story of love that identifies no borders, no religion and no castes, and attains its bliss after twenty-two long years of silent endurance and sacrifice. Directed by Yash Chopra, this blockbuster movie depicts a romance set against the ongoing conflict between India and Pakistan. Backed with a touching story and powerful performances, this movie instantly broke box-office records for the year worldwide.

There have been several movies in the past that dealt with the disturbed relations between India and Pakistan. But while other movies talked about the antagonism between these two countries, *Veer-Zaara* proclaimed the essential similarities between them as against the artificially created differences and urged for the need to recognize our mutual brotherhood.

One of the highlights of the movie is the cameo performances by Amitabh Bachchan and Hema Malini. These two senior actors managed to leave a strong imprint on the movie despite their small roles. The movie is also a comeback of sorts for Yash Chopra. His last directorial venture before this film was *Dil To Pagal Hai* (1997). He returned after eight years to direct *Veer-Zaara*.

Another speciality of the movie is its music which is based on the compositions by the late Madan Mohan, as revised by his son, Sanjeev Kohli. The songs thus produced soar high with their haunting melodies and throb with an irresistible passion of love.

Memorable songs of **Veer Zara**

Song	*Singers*
Tere liye	Lata Mangeshkar and Roop Kumar Rathod
Main yahan hoon	Udit Narayan
Aisa des hai mera	Lata Mangeshkar, Udit Narayan, Gurdas Mann and Pritha Majumdar
Yeh hum aa gaye hain kahan	Lata Mangeshkar and Udit Narayan
Do pal	Lata Mangeshkar and Sonu Nigam
Kyon hawa	Lata Mangeshkar and Sonu Nigam, commentary by Yash Chopra
Hum to bhai jaise hain	Lata Mangeshkar
Aaya tere dar par	Ahmed Hussain and Mohd. Hussain
Lo aa gayi lo di ve	Lata Mangeshkar, Udit Narayan and Gurdas Mann
Tum paas aa rahe ho	Jagjit Singh and Lata Mangeshkar
Jaane Kyon	Lata Mangeshkar

Most of the story is told in flashback from Veer's prison cell. Squadron Leader Veer Pratap Singh (Shahrukh Khan) is a rescue pilot with the Indian Air Force, who risks his own life to

save the lives of others. Zaara Haayat Khan (Preity Zinta) is a Pakistani girl travelling to India. She is a carefree, sprightly daughter of a Pakistani politician and has come to India to fulfil her surrogate mother's dying wish. Her bus meets with an accident and she is rescued by Squadron Leader Veer Pratap Singh (Shahrukh Khan). He is struck by her beauty and knows that his life would never be the same again. He helps Zaara fulfil the dying wish of her *Bebe* and then takes her on a tour of India's Punjab as well as to his village where his Bauji Chaudhury Sumer Singh (Amitabh Bachchan) and Maati Saraswati Kaur (Hema Malini) live.

Veer falls deeply in love with Zaara but before he could propose to her, it is revealed that Zaara is engaged to another man, Raza (Manoj Bajpai). Veer nevertheless confesses his love, and then watches sadly as Zaara boards the train that will take her back to Pakistan. Both believe that this is the end of their story.

But Veer's parting words of love and the memories of the moments spent in his company continue to haunt Zaara. She eventually realizes that she loves Veer and cannot marry anyone else. She's traumatized by her love and longing for Veer. Her maid and friend Shabbo (Divya Dutta) cannot see her suffering and makes a phone call to India, urging Veer to come to Pakistan and rescue Zaara from the forced marriage.

Veer doesn't think twice before leaving his job and travelling to Pakistan to find his love. He meets her in a mosque and Zaara, overcome by her emotions, hugs him in front of everybody, thus creating a scandal and offending her fiancé. Her

father is so hurt by her action that he becomes seriously ill. Her mother begs Veer to leave Zaara. Zaara's father is a high-profile politician whose reputation will be ruined if news got out that his daughter is in love with an Indian. Veer respects the request of her mother and decides to leave Pakistan. Zaara too decides to sacrifice her love for the wishes of her parents. But Zaara's fiancé, outraged by the shame Zaara has brought upon him, frames Veer and has him wrongly imprisoned for being an Indian spy named Raj Rathore. He threatens to sully Zaara's reputation if Veer denies the charges against him. In order to protect Zaara, Veer silently accepts every accusation and is thrown in the jailime passes and Veer is now an old and broken-down man, still languishing in a Pakistani jail, steadfastly protecting Zaara's honour by remaining mute against all the false charges levied against him.

The story takes a turn with the entry of Saamiya Siddiqui (Rani Mukerji). She is an idealistic Pakistani lawyer, whose mission in life is to pave the path for women's empowerment. To dissuade a female lawyer from being successful, she has been given Veer's case as her first independent case. It is considered an impossible case by all.

By this time, it's been twenty-two years since Veer has been in prison. He hasn't spoken to anyone all these years. Saamiya makes it her mission to discover the truth about Veer and see to it that justice is served. And thus starts her journey to unveil the truth, the story of Veer and his life. Veer is assigned the number 786 as his prisoner identity number in the Pakistani jail. According to Islam, 786 is a sacred number. This convinces Saamiya that Veer is a person loved by Allah. He must, therefore, be true and honest. Veer tells Saamiya to do anything for the case except mention Zaara's family. He believes that Veer and Zaara are not destined to be together. But Saamiya vows to change that and to unite them together and forever.

Saamiya goes to Veer's village in India to gather evidence to prove that Veer is the real Squadron Leader Veer Pratap Singh and not any spy called Raj Rathore. There, she is surprised to find Zaara and her friend Shabbo (Divya Dutta). It is revealed that after Veer was put in prison, the bus by which he should have been travelling back to India had met with an accident and everyone in it had died. And since nobody knew about Raza's treachery, it had been assumed that Veer too had died in the accident. Zaara had been so heart-broken by this news that her father herself had freed her of the forced marriage and given her leave to go to India and serve Veer's family and village. And so, she had been living in India for all the twenty-two years while Veer in Pakistan had been guarding her reputation with his silence against all atrocities, believing her to be married to Raza and living a happy married life.

Saamiya brings her back to Pakistan to testify in favour of Veer. He is exonerated. Veer and Zaara go back to India, united finally in the sacred bond of matrimony after the separation of twenty-two long years.

 *Remarks*

❂ *Veer-Zaara* was featured in the February 2005 issue of the National Geographic Magazine in an article about Bollywood.

❂ The film was a success not only in India and Pakistan, but overseas, notably in United Kingdom, Germany, France, South Africa and the United States. When the three Indian stars, Shah Rukh, Preity and Rani, visited the Virgin Megastore in the UK, over 5,000 fans thronged the store.

❂ On April 26, 2006, *Veer-Zaara* had its French premiere at The Grand Rex, the biggest theatre in Paris. *Veer-Zaara* is the first Hindi film to premiere in such a large venue.

The film was originally going to be called *Yeh Kahaan Aa Gaye Hum*, a name taken from the title of a song in the movie *Silsila* (1981). The director, Yash Chopra, eventually decided on *Veer-Zaara* as a title. However, one of the songs in the film is called *Yeh hum aa gaye hain kahan*, a twist on the proposed title.

The role of Saamiya Siddiqui was originally intended for Aishwarya Rai, but it did not work out.

Awards

National Awards

- Best Popular Film Providing Wholesome Entertainment

Filmfare Awards

- Best Movie
- Best Actor-Shahrukh Khan
- Best Lyricist - Javed Akhtar for '*Tere Liye*'
- Best Dialogue - Aditya Chopra
- Best Story - Aditya Chopra

IIFA Awards

- Best Movie
- Best Director - Yash Chopra
- Best Actor - Shahrukh Khan
- Best Supporting Actress - Rani Mukerji
- Best Music Director - The Late Madan Mohan and Sanjeev Kohli.

Stardust Awards

- Star of the Year - Female - Preity Zinta

Screen Awards

- Best Film
- Best Actor - Shahrukh Khan
- Best Dialogue - Aditya Chopra
- Best Story -Aditya Chopra
- Best Jodi No.1 - Shah Rukh Khan and Preity Zinta
- Best Supporting Actor
- Best Lyrics
- Best Screenplay
- Best Cinematography

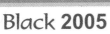

Black **2005**

Director	●	Sanjay Leela Bhansali
Producer	●	Sanjay Leela Bhansali (Bhansali Productions)
Story	●	Sanjay Leela Bhansali,
	●	Bhawani Iyer
	●	Prakash Kapadia
Starring	●	Amitabh Bachchan...as Debraj Sahai
	●	Rani Mukherjee........as Michelle McNally
	●	Ayesha Kapoor...as Young Michelle McNally
	●	Shernaz Patel...........as Catherine McNally
	●	Dhritiman Chatterjee ..as Paul McNally
	●	Nandana Sen........... as Sarah McNally
	●	Sillo Mahava............as Mrs. Gomes
	●	Mahabanoo Mody-Kotwal..as Mrs. Nair
Music	●	Monty Sharma
Distributed by	●	Yash Raj Films
Release date(s)	●	February 4, 2005
Running time	●	122 min
Language		Hindi/Urdu/English (colour)

Black released in 2005, glowed bright in its very *blackness* and thundered through the award functions, gathering in its sweep every major film award for that year. This story of a blind and deaf girl was directed by Sanjay Leela Bhansali and brought to life by the superb performances of Amitabh Bachchan, Rani Mukerji and the child actress Ayesha Kapoor. There's no song in this movie, but still the entire film succeeds in maintaining a tenacious grasp over the viewer by its subtle drama, brilliant screenplay, mesmerizing performances and awesome cinematography.

The film is based on the life of Helen Keller. In fact, the first half is very similar to the 1962 film *The Miracle Worker,* which focuses on Anne Sullivan's struggle to educate Helen Keller. *Black*, however, is not just a story of a blind and deaf girl. It is a story of endurance, self-belief, and of letting a light shine even through the most impregnable darkness.

 Story

The film starts when the blind and deaf Michelle (Rani Mukerji) runs into her aged, ailing and dying teacher Debraj (Amitabh Bachchan). From there begins, in flashback, the unfolding of the long, hard struggle that they had fought together, and won, defeating with their indomitable determination the very handicaps that had bound her in.

Michelle McNally loses her eyesight and hearing at the tender age of eighteen months, causing her to grow up in a world where she is isolated in the darkness of her own existence. She understands nothing of the frustrating world around her and grows up to be a violent, uncontrollable eight-year old. Her parents, Paul and Catherine, are at their wits' end, until Debraj Sahai enters their lives. An elderly alcoholic teacher for the deaf and blind, Debraj is a disillusioned, eccentric man who sees himself as a magician. He takes it upon himself to bring young Michelle into the light- the light of knowledge and of awareness of the world around her. It's a long journey, full of disappointments and defeats. But their long endurance pays and Michelle, after struggling for several years, succeeds in fulfilling her teacher's dream by graduating from a *normal* college.

 Remarks

- A fire broke out on the sets at Mumbai's Film City during the making of this film. Four fire engines were required to put out the fire.

- Rani Mukerji wore dark-tinted contact lenses to squint and cross her eyes as required for the role.

- At first, Rani Mukerji refused to step in, because she felt that she was unable to play the character she was asked to. But once she agreed, she managed to give what is perhaps her most stellar performance till date.

- Sanjay Leela Bhansali named the film after his favourite color.

- The movie's title was originally registered with Kumar Gaurav. Sanjay Leela Bhansali approached him and requested him to relinquish the title, as he wanted it for his movie. Kumar felt that Bhansali's film was bold and path breaking and agreed to render any help that he could to the film. Sanjay has duly acknolwdged his gratitude to Kumar Gaurav in the opening credits of his film.

- Unusual for a work by Bhansali, there are no songs or dance sequences featured in this film. So, the background score became of paramount importance to the composer, Monty. To create more of an uplifting aura for the deaf-blind-mute character of Michelle McNally, he used pianos and strings, but kept the voices in the chorus at a low octave.

- The film is based on screenwriter Prakash Kapadia's Gujarati play *Aatam Vinjhe Paankh*, which was inspired from *The Miracle Worker.*

- Director Bhansali hoped to make a film that was an extension of his critically acclaimed debut film *Khamoshi : The Musical* (1996). Both were based on a visit he made to the Helen Keller Institute.

Awards

National Award

- 2005: Best Actor (Amitabh Bachchan)
- 2005: Best feature film in Hindi

Filmfare Awards

- *Black* established a record at the Filmfare Awards by bagging eleven awards.
- Best Film
- Best Director- Sanjay Leela Bhansali
- Best Actor- Amitabh Bachchan
- Best Actress - Rani Mukerji
- Critics Award Best Film - Sanjay Leela Bhansali
- Critics Award BestPerformance - Amitabh Bachchan and Rani Mukerji (each)
- Best Supporting Actress - Ayesha Kapoor
- Best Editing - Bela Sehgal
- Best Cinematography - Ravi K. Chandran
- Best Background Score - Monty Sharma

IIFA Awards

- Best Film
- Best Director - Sanjay Leela Bhansali
- Best Actor - Amitabh Bachchan
- Best Actress - Rani Mukerji
- Best Supporting Actress - Ayesha Kapur
- Best Cinematography - Ravi K. Chandran
- Best Editing - Bela Sehgal
- Best Sound Recording - Anup Dev
- Best Background Score - Monty Sharma

Screen Awards

- Best Film
- Best Director - Sanjay Leela Bhansali
- Best Actor - Amitabh Bachchan
- Best Actress - Rani Mukerji

- Best Supporting Actress - Ayesha Kapur
- Best Cinematography - Ravi K. Chandran
- Best Editing - Bela Sehgal
- Best Sound Recording - Anup Dev
- Best Background Score - Monty Sharma

ZEE Cine Awards

- Best Film
- Best Director - Sanjay Leela Bhansali
- Best Actor - Amitabh Bachchan
- Best Actress - Rani Mukerji
- Best Supporting Actress - Ayesha Kapur
- Best Cinematography - Ravi K. Chandran
- Best Editing - Bela Sehgal
- Best Sound Recording - Anup Dev
- Best Background Score - Monty Sharma

Other Awards

- 2006, Stardust Star of the Year Award Female
- 2006, Star's Sabsey Favourite Heroine
- 2005, The Lycra® MTV Style Awards Most Stylish in Films
- 2006, Bengal Film Journalists' Association Awards, Best Actress (HindiMovies)
- 2006, Sony Film Jury Best Actress of the Year
- 2006, Rediff Movie Awards Best Actress
- 2006, 2nd Apsara Awards Best Actress
- 2006, Idea Zee Fashion Awards Celebrity Model of the Year FM's Best Actress
- 2005, Anandolok Puroshkar Awards Best Actress
- 2005, Bollywood Fashion Awards Celebrity Style Female Award
- 2005, Lion Awards Achievement in Cinema
- 2006, National film awards Winner Best Actor

BOOT POLISH
BOOB PRODUCTIONS PRIVATE LIMITED
KUMAR · NARGIS · RAJ KAPOOR

SHOLAY

Preeti Zinta
ZAARA HAYAAT KHAN

vash chopra's
VEER-ZAARA

NDAZ

The Perfect Indian Film
MUGHAL-E-AZAM

GURU DUTT FILMS LTD.
PYAASA

BOLLYWOOD
ENTERTAINMENT

DOLBY
DIGITAL

BLACK

MOTHE
INDIA

HRISHIKESH MUKHERJEE'S
Anand

Hum Aapke